W9-CUQ-789

"Differentiation is absolutely essential in today's competitive job market, and Kristen Jacoway's book provides practical strategies for setting yourself apart and attracting the attention of hiring managers. In 'I'm in a Job Search—Now What???,' Jacoway reminds us that career success today requires understanding your personal brand and integrating that brand into everything you do."
William Arruda, Founder of Reach Personal Branding and Author of 'Career Distinction: Stand Out by Building Your Brand'

"We're in the midst of a Social Media Revolution that's changing how we live, do business—and yes, how we look for jobs! If you're a job seeker who knows social media is key to career success, but are reluctant to get started, then this book is for you! By relating her personal experiences and learning, as well as her professional career coaching experience, author Kristen Jacoway guides you with clear instruction, as well as insider tips, on how to take your job search beyond your résumé and job boards! In her book, Kristen starts you off with setting up a career planning roadmap, and then helps you fill in the details with guidance that includes personal branding, online identity, effective use of social media like LinkedIn, Facebook, Twitter, and YouTube—and much more! So, if you want to get started in managing your career online—and you should—let Kristen show you the way!"
Walter Akana, Career/Life Strategist, Threshold Consulting, http://www.threshold-consulting.com

"Looking for a job? In transition? If you need a fast, easy-to-read, informative guide to achieve your career search goals, Kristen Jacoway's 'I'm in a Job Search—Now What???' is a great place to start. Information-packed with plenty of exercises to jumpstart your job search, it serves as a valuable reference guide—both for those just starting out and for seasoned careerists. With its overview of personal branding, social media, and job search strategies and resources, it can serve as your central hub for planning and executing a search that works for you. If time is of the essence, read this must-have career book now!"
Tara Kachaturoff, Producer and Host, Michigan Entrepreneur TV, http://www.MichiganEntrepreneurTV.com

"'...career management is a ramp and not a ladder where you can stop and rest for a bit.' And this is exactly why Kristen's book is such a great read. It fosters the mindset of perpetual motion in proactively managing your career. Created in workbook form so you can make notes, follow the steps, and complete goals, candidates can quickly and effectively launch a balanced search strategy. The SWOT analysis for leveraging company research is well worth the purchase price!"
Cindy Kraft, CFO-Coach, Executive Essentials, Tampa, FL, USA

"'I'm in a Job Search—Now What???' is a must for every professional looking to accelerate their job search and generate serious results. Kristen uses engaging exercises to coach you through an otherwise challenging process so you can customize the plan for your unique situation. As a Personal Branding Strategist, Kristen will help you identify a competitive branding message and coach you on the use of social media to connect you with industry experts and targeted employers. Not only will this high-impact duo help deliver immediate results, but these strategies will help you implement long-term career management and resiliency strategies that will benefit your career for years to come."
Valerie Plis, Master Certified Career Coach,
http://www.ExceedWithPurposeCoaching.com

"Kristen Jacoway's 'I'm in a Job Search—Now What???' provides a clear step-by-step process for managing your job search. It not only provides great information about clarifying your personal brand, your online identity, your career marketing materials, social media and online networking, but also includes exercises to help you start applying the learning and taking action right away. A great book for the job seeker looking to embrace the power of the online world to accelerate their job search."
Megan Fitzgerald, Expat Career and Personal Branding Coach,
http://www.careerbychoice.com

I'm in a Job Search—Now What??? (2nd Edition)

By Kristen Jacoway
Foreword by Jason Alba

20660 Stevens Creek Blvd., Suite 210
Cupertino, CA 95014

Published by Happy About®
20660 Stevens Creek Blvd., Suite 210, Cupertino, CA 95014
http://happyabout.com

Second Edition: June 2012
First Edition: January 2010
Paperback ISBN (Second Edition): 978-1-60005-226-2
(1-60005-226-6)
Paperback ISBN (First Edition): 978-1-60005-170-8 (1-60005-170-7)
eBook ISBN (Second Edition): 978-1-60005-227-9 (1-60005-227-4)
eBook ISBN (First Edition): 978-1-60005-171-5 (1-60005-171-5)
Place of Publication: Silicon Valley, California, USA
Paperback Library of Congress Number: 2009938534

Trademarks

Warning and Disclaimer

Acknowledgments

First, I want to thank my Executive Editor, Jason Alba, because without him, this book would still be in my head instead of on paper. He encouraged me to write it and has been a tremendous resource to me. I couldn't have done it without his help, Mitchell Levy, Liz Tadman, and the great publishing staff at Happy About.

I'd also like to thank Rachel Gogos, http://www.thebrandid.com, for helping me brainstorm the title of the book.

Thanks also to my friends and family, fans of my business page on Facebook, and people on Twitter who supported and cheered me along the way.

A special thanks to my parents, Gene and Judith Austin. To my children, Russell and Emma—I love you both and I appreciate the time you gave me to fulfill my dream of writing a book that I hope helps many, many people in a career transition.

A Message from Happy About®

Thank you for your purchase of this Happy About book. It is available online at http://www.happyabout.com/jobsearchnowwhat.php or at other online and physical bookstores.

- Please contact us for quantity discounts at sales@happyabout.info
- If you want to be informed by email of upcoming Happy About® books, please email bookupdate@happyabout.info

Happy About is interested in you if you are an author who would like to submit a non-fiction book proposal or a corporation that would like to have a book written for you. Please contact us by email editorial@happyabout.info or phone (1-408-257-3000).

Other Happy About books available include:

- Happy About My Resume:
  http://www.happyabout.com/myresume.php
- #JOBSEARCH tweet Book01:
  http://www.happyabout.com/thinkaha/jobsearchtweet01.php
- Happy About The Career Alphabet:
  http://www.happyabout.com/happyaboutcareeralphabet.php
- Internet Your Way to a New Job:
  http://www.happyabout.com/InternetYourWaytoaNewJob.php
- I'm at a Networking Event—Now What???:
  http://www.happyabout.com/networking-event.php
- Storytelling about Your Brand Online & Offline:
  http://www.happyabout.com/storytelling.php
- I'm on LinkedIn—Now What???(3rd Edition):
  http://www.happyabout.com/linkedinhelp.php
- The Successful Introvert:
  http://www.happyabout.com/thesuccessfulintrovert.php
- Turbocharged Networking For $100K+ Jobs:
  http://www.happyabout.com/turbochargednetworking.php
- Fast Track Guide to a Professional Job Search:
  http://www.happyabout.com/fasttrackjobsearch.php
- #ENTRYLEVELtweet Book01:
  http://www.happyabout.com/thinkaha/entryleveltweet01.php
- #ENTRYLEVELtweet Book02:
  http://www.happyabout.com/thinkaha/entryleveltweet02.php

Contents

Foreword by Jason Alba

As a rule, I decided to not write any forewords on any Now What??? books, simply because it seemed I should not be the one writing them for authors I was coaching through the process. In fact, I suggested that Kristen ask a number of other career experts to write the foreword, and even offered to facilitate the introductions. But it kept coming back to me, and I finally agreed.

Why?

Because this book is different—it is near and dear to my professional life and my own business. You see, a few years ago, I was in my first involuntary transition and extremely frustrated. I was too busy spinning my wheels in a fruitless job search to step back and try and figure out what I was doing wrong.

My assumptions on how to do a job search were grossly wrong then, and even worse now. So much has changed from when I came out of school—back then you could almost count on job boards to be a significant part of your job search. And there was this notion or expectation of being with a company for a long time.

Today, job boards can't be a significant part of your job search, and no company is quick to hint you'll be around for a very long time. That's where this book comes in. Kristen shares strategies and tactics any job seeker could employ—from traditional résumés to standard social networking to how to use YouTube in a job search. Kristen lays the foundation to help you understand the principles, tells you where to go to implement them, and then shares the tactics of how to do it.

Once you have a foundation, the tactics are key. Some tactics will apply to you, others might not. The good news is you have a lot of information here, and you should be ready to get to work. The bad news is there isn't a job offer waiting in the pages of this book, but doing what Kristen prescribes can help you achieve a level of career management that you might not have thought about.

Don't make the costly mistake I made in my job search and assume you know how to implement a job search—my assumptions were outdated and ineffective. Weigh your situation against what Kristen shares here and you should see a change in your job search as well as your overall career management.

Jason Alba
CEO, JibberJobber.com
(http://www.JibberJobber.com)
Author of 'I'm on LinkedIn—Now What???'
(http://www.imonlinkedinnowwhat.com)
Creator of LinkedIn for Job Seekers, the DVD
(http://www.linkedinforjobseekers.com)

My former husband has been in two job searches. He worked for a company for twenty years. The company, like most manufacturing companies, had to offshore manufacturing to remain competitive. We found a new job through networking and he started that position before his old job was moved overseas. Nearly eighteen months later, that company closed the doors.

In the first career transition, we had his résumé professionally rewritten. We loved the results and both of us felt that it was the silver bullet for him getting his next position. We applied to job after job on an executive job board, and after a few months into the job search, were disheartened that we'd had no bites. We submitted his beautiful résumé to hundreds of recruiters and again were shocked that no one contacted him.

I had worked several years as a vocational counselor in the 1990s. After my former husband started working in his new position in 2007, I trained with some of the industry experts in career coaching, personal branding, and online identity and earned five additional career certifications. The information I learned in my training strikes such a sharp contrast to how we conducted job searches in the past. After I completed my training, I clearly understood how misguided our efforts were in his first career transition. In today's environment, *multiple* strategies are required to land your next position. You can't depend on just a well-written résumé or applying to a job board or blasting your résumé to multiple recruiters. You must market yourself in many ways to support your résumé, job applications, and relationship with recruiters in today's job market.

This book is written by someone who has been in your shoes and knows the stressors that so frustrate a job seeker. It is my hope that I will provide you with resources and ideas that will facilitate and fast-track your job searching efforts.

My book is really not just for people in a career transition, but also for people who have a position. We live in a time where people don't climb ladders anymore. People are on a ramp with their career management, and unlike a ladder where you might be able to stop for a rest, a ramp requires constant movement to maintain your position and advance.

In this title, we will explore some of the newest avenues in seeking employment, including utilizing Twitter, Facebook, LinkedIn, Video Social Networking Platforms, etc., as well as some traditional approaches. We will begin by determining goals and finding out what is distinctive and special about you and how to leverage your unique promise of value in career marketing. Then, prepare to launch your brand on the Internet to build on-brand, relevant results so that when a recruiter or hiring manager googles your name, they will discover the multi-faceted aspects of what makes you different from everyone else. In December 2010, Microsoft commissioned a study and found that 79% of hiring managers and job recruiters Google potential candidates. In this same study, they found that 70% have admitted to rejecting a candidate based on their findings.[1]

During your time of transition from unemployment to employment, we will focus on some things you can do in the interim that will help you in your job search. It is a difficult time, but to succeed in a job search, you must be willing to use multiple job searching strategies and commit to the time needed to pursue employment opportunities. It is a full-time job in and of itself.

I am an avid believer in utilizing multiple marketing and search strategies to find a job. People have to know, like, and trust you before offering you a position. Social media is providing professionals in a job search with tools unlike we've ever known. Social media provides a free or low-cost platform to give you the opportunity to "sell" your skills to a potential employer. Using social media as **part** of your job search marketing plan can leverage the ACT-B model in your strategy. ACT-B means—**A** is *awareness* of who you are and what you can offer; **C** is having enough available content for someone to *consider*; **T** is letting people see a *trial* of what you can do; and then **B** is the *buy* when someone offers you a job.

---

1. Cross-tab Transforming Market Research, "Online Reputation in a Connected World," January 2010, http://tinyurl.com/7vfv279 (accessed April 29, 2012).

Throughout this book, you will see notes to let you know that you can enter the information into JibberJobber. JibberJobber (http://www.jibberjobber.com) was created by Jason Alba. Jason was laid off from his company and developed this dynamic career management tool. You can organize and manage your job search; maintain a database of networking contacts, recruiters, and companies; you can track jobs to which you've applied; read articles on career management in his library; and of course, follow his blog for tips, resources, and ideas. JibberJobber has a free membership and a paid membership. You can review the differences on his website to decide which one will work best for you.

1 Roadmap for Career Planning

This book provides you with many strategies and gives a workbook approach to your overall career transition. I designed a roadmap to introduce you to the journey we are about to take. The roadmap was created to give you an overview of what will be discussed in the book and how you can go from point to point in your job search strategies. The appendix gives most of the 100+ resources listed throughout the book in one, easy-to-find place.

Goals—First, define your career goals for both short- and long-term.

Personal Branding—Second, determine your personal brand to see how you are unique from everyone else who has your same job title. What are your strengths, your team and leadership roles, and so on?

Online Identity—Check your online identity to see what employers, recruiters, and hiring managers find when they google your name. Do the results paint a consistent story about your strengths and expertise?

Build Your Visibility on Google—Your visibility on Google is an important step since most employers, recruiters, and hiring managers will google you before contacting you. We will look at five strategies to build your results and portray your personal brand for your digital footprint.

Target/Research Companies Where You Want to Work—Develop a list of companies in your geographic preference where you'd like to work. Use the research tools provided to find companies that are within a certain radius of your zip code, company size (how many employees, how much revenues, and so forth), industry, etc.

Next, visit the company websites of your targeted companies. Do they have job postings on their website? If possible, set an RSS feed or an email alert on positions of interest.

Develop Your Career Marketing Material—Write a branded résumé that is customized for each position for which you apply. Develop a cover letter that shows not only your interest, but also your knowledge about the company. Demonstrate how you are the best fit for a position by using a customized strategy on your cover letter. Create business cards, online and offline, for networking events and online platforms. Follow up with a thank-you note after an interview.

Leverage Social Media—You can use social media platforms, such as LinkedIn, Twitter, Facebook, and Pinterest, to create a professional profile that is searchable to employers, recruiters, and hiring managers. Social media also creates a platform for you to forge and maintain networking contacts within your industry. Networking is one of the biggest keys to your career transition success!

Additionally, LinkedIn, Facebook, and Twitter post jobs; this gives you access to job postings that may be exclusive to these three platforms.

Network in Person—Maintain your existing network and find events to expand it. Find ways to help others in your network and remember that networking is ongoing. You need to network when you are in a position AND when you are in a career transition.

Understand How to Relate and Work with Recruiters—I interviewed Jeff Lipschultz, Principal of A-List Solutions and a recruiter. He gives valuable information on how best to work with a recruiter. Remember, recruiters fill positions for companies. They are not looking for positions for you.

Identify Vertical Job Boards and Niche Job Boards—Again, set up RSS feeds and email alerts to let you know when a job matching your criteria is posted. Automate this process as much as possible and spend your time on other multiple strategies for your career transition.

Prepare for Your Interview—I provide instructions for you to learn the type of information you need to research prior to your interview and how to best prepare for the types of questions you might encounter.

Wash, Rinse, and Repeat—Remember that career management is a ramp and not a ladder where you can stop and rest for a bit. Maintain your network online and offline, keep a journal of achievements for updating your résumé, stay in touch with your recruiter(s), build on-brand results on Google, and check in on how you are progressing towards your ultimate career goal. Always be ready for change!

2 Setting Goals

First things first. Have you written your goals for your job search? What are your long-term goals and where do you see yourself at retirement? What are the steps you will need to achieve to reach these objectives? Developing a job search marketing plan requires that you set goals for yourself. When you decide upon your goals and supporting goals, write them down, and post them in a place where you can see them every day.

What is your long-term objective?

Make sure that your long-term and short-term goals follow the S.M.A.R.T. (believed to have been coined by Peter Drucker in 1954) rule of thumb:

S - Specific

M - Measurable

A - Attainable

R - Realistic

T - Timeframe Specific

One of my favorite quotes is: "It is a paradoxical but profoundly true and important principle of life that the most likely way to reach a goal is to be aiming not at that goal itself but at some more ambitious goal beyond it." – Arnold Toynbee[2]

If you have a more ambitious goal for which you are aiming, you are not placing limits on what it is you can achieve.

I actually wrote my S.M.A.R.T. goal for writing this 2nd Edition book and getting it published, as well as delivering twelve workshops this year. I have them written and saved as my screensaver so I can see them each and every day to be reminded of my goals. For example, here is how I've broken down writing a book:

> *Contact publisher(s) to pitch idea*
> *Secure contract*
> *Goal for book length is more than 20,000 words*
> *Write at least 200 words every day for 100 days*
> *Send draft to the editor by my deadline of April 25, 2012*

It is specific because I know my title and the ideas I want included. It is measurable because I have broken down how many words I will write per day. The book is attainable and realistic because I have many blog posts, reference files, email answers, content from speeches and trainings, and years of experience as a career counselor that I can pull together to serve as resource material for the book. My goal is timeframe specific as I aimed to have the first draft to the editor by April 25, 2012. By the way, I presented eight workshops in a seven-month period of time.

The Other Half of S.M.A.R.T. Goals

If you have written your goals to match the S.M.A.R.T. rules, then you've done half the work. What's the other half? Knowing the reason and purpose of WHY you have set these goals. Are the reasons and

---

2. Arnold Toynbee, "Quotations by Author," The Quotations Page, http://www.quotationspage.com/quotes/Arnold_Toynbee/ (accessed August 26, 2009).

purposes enough to propel you forward to achieve these goals? Furthermore, how many times have you set these goals for yourself only to fail to achieve them?

First, you must take a look at the underlying belief you have established about accomplishing these goals. For example, if you achieve X then Y will happen. Does Y contain the elements to make you want to commit to your goal? If not, why?

Now, if these underlying beliefs are what have prevented you from being successful in the past, what changes can you make in your belief system to achieve your goals? If you changed the belief that job searching equals pain and frustration to one that job searching will energize you and open up new opportunities that are more exciting than your previous job, would you be motivated now? You know it could happen, but changing the BELIEF system from unconsciously associating it with pain and frustration to associating it with energy, new opportunities, new avenues, excitement, and satisfaction is what will propel you forward.

Are your goals S.M.A.R.T.? What are your beliefs about your goals? Do you need to change any of your unconscious beliefs to achieve the goals of the past that have been broken repeatedly? Write down your reasons, any associated beliefs, and the beliefs you MUST have to be successful during this career transition!

So many people give up on their goals because they mess up one or two days and they resonate the message, "I can't do it—I always mess up—why even try?" Be accountable to someone for your goals and remember that we all fall short from time to time. Persevere and realize that you are going to have a bad day now and then. Look at what got in your way that day and what supports you can put in place to keep that obstacle from reappearing.

One reason coaching is so effective for people is because during coaching, you set the agenda for the goals you want to attain and your coach helps you to come up with actionable items to achieve these targets. Most coaches will end the session by asking you for what you will be accountable for the following session. If you don't succeed in accomplishing those actionable items, your coach helps you to determine what obstacles prevented you from accomplishing these actionable items and will help you brainstorm ways to not let these road bumps get in your way again. If you are successful, your coach will celebrate your success with you through supportive words, or an e-card. If you can't afford coaching, find a trusted friend or someone to whom you can be accountable and who will hold you answerable.

I've covered some material that may be new to you, while some material may just be a refresher for you. In any case, I hope that you are beginning to see the importance of setting goals. Goals give you direction and form the roadmap to help you achieve your objectives.

I was a vocational rehabilitation counselor for many years and we used to help our clients write out Individualized Written Rehabilitation Programs. We stated the vocational goal/objective, the resources to help attain that goal, the start date, the date to re-evaluate, the approximate end date, and the evaluation criterion. I have helped more than 400 people write these plans. Contained in these plans are the components to writing your own goals.

Goals Change Direction

What happens if you set goals for yourself and work hard, but something happens that keeps you from reaching a particular goal? What should you do? Reassess, look ahead, and envision a new goal to help you reach your ultimate vision. Sometimes we have a goal that for some reason or another doesn't work and is not achieved. Should we give up? No! See if there are other ways to reach that goal or ascertain if that goal was attainable. At times, we have visions that may not work quite the way we thought they might, but actually are reached in a different way.

For example, I heard a speaker tell the story of Mary McLeod Bethune, an African American, who was born in 1875 in South Carolina. She was the fifteenth of the seventeen children born to Samuel and Patsy McLeod, who were both former slaves. Many of her siblings were born into slavery. She demonstrated a desire to learn to read and write, and attended a one-room schoolhouse, Trinity Missions School. Her vision was to be a missionary in Africa and teach school. She worked very hard to reach this goal, but was told after years of hard study that her application was not accepted because missionaries who were African American were not needed.

Did she stop? Not a chance! She re-evaluated and decided a different way to reach her vision of teaching. If she couldn't teach in Africa, she could still reach her dream and teach in the U.S. In 1904, she opened a school for girls in Daytona Beach, FL and had six students. She made desks out of crates and obtained supplies from charity. Bethune, the parents of the students, and the church members raised money by making sweet potato pies, ice cream, and fried fish, and selling them to construction crews. Pencils were made from burned wood. She also recruited wealthy business people to sit on the board, including James Gamble of Procter & Gamble and Thomas White of White Sewing Machines. She raised funds for the school by talking to people like John D. Rockfeller who gave her a $62,000 donation in 1905.

By 1910, six short years later, the enrollment had risen to 102. By 1920, the school's value was appraised at $100,000 and the enrollment had risen to 351 students. In 1923, the school merged with the Cookman Institute for Men and became co-educational. In 2004, Bethune-Cookman University celebrated its 100-year anniversary.[3]

When obstacles appear, don't give up hope—dream another way to fulfill your ultimate vision. Look at people like Bethune who had enormous hurdles to overcome—and remember success leaves clues.

Job Search Frustration and How Goals Can Help

The reason I started this book with setting goals (even if they are mini-goals) is because many people become frustrated with their job search. My former husband has experienced frustration from time to time. Goals give you direction on action items you need to do each day

---

3. Wikipedia, "Mary McLeod Bethune," Wikipedia, August 25, 2009, http://en.wikipedia.org/wiki/Mary_McLeod_Bethune (accessed August 26, 2009).

to reach your ultimate goal. If you can make strides towards achieving these goals and are seeing progress, this will hopefully not seem as daunting or overwhelming as it can when you have no plan.

When you have no plan, how do you go about your day? Most people just spend time on things that are not moving them forward towards their goal. I know when I purposely plan items that will move me towards my goal each day, I feel a sense of control and accomplishment—I definitely feel, at the end of the day, that I'm one step closer. When I don't plan, I end up wondering what happened to my day and realizing that I didn't do what was needed to attain my goal.

I understand how being frustrated can leave you unmotivated. I'd really encourage you to listen or read something motivational on a daily basis. Many books, podcasts, webcasts, and so on are published on this very subject. Some of my favorite books include 'The How of Happiness' by Sonja Lyubomirsky and 'The 4:8 Principle: The Secret to a Joy-Filled Life' by Tommy Newberry.

Let's focus on setting goals and steps to reach those goals. Your first call to action for this book is to complete this part of your job marketing plan. We'll be filling in other areas as we go through the book. By the time you've completed this book, you should have a working job search marketing plan.

Career Objective/Goal:

_____

Purpose of the goal/Why you want this goal (List all your reasons and make sure they are compelling enough to drive you forward.):

_____
_____
_____
_____
_____
_____

Resources that can help (List who and what can help you—family, friends, continuing education class, etc.):

_____

_____

_____

_____

_____

_____

Start date:

_____

How often are you going to evaluate your progress? (This might be daily, weekly, or monthly—determine what's best for you.)

_____

Evaluation criterion (How are you going to MEASURE your success?):

_____

_____

_____

3 What's Your Google Quotient and Personal Brand?

Today, people are going to google you before interviewing you or deciding if you are the right person with whom to do business. So, we need to get a baseline of where you fall in the quadrant of digital distinction. You want to understand what sets you apart from your competition (i.e., your personal brand) and how to build results on Google that are branded and relevant to your area of expertise. In the next chapter, I will take you through five different strategies that you can implement. Let's get started!

Reach Communications (http://www.reachpersonalbranding.com) has developed a free tool called the *Online Identity Calculator* (http://www.onlineidcalculator.com) to help you determine if you are **Digitally Disguised**, **Digitally Disastrous**, **Digitally Dabbling**, or the coveted **Digitally Distinct**.

First, you will be asked to enter your name and email address to start the process. The system uses this email to send you your results.

Next, you will complete your profile. As it says in the profile area, they aggregate these responses for backend data for writing articles, press releases, and their next book. They firmly state that your responses are NOT associated with your email address.

You will answer a series of questions after you enter your name in quotation marks for a Google search (for example, "Kristen Jacoway"). After you answer these questions, you will click the button marked "Calculate My Online Identity" and will be directed to a page that plots your results on a graph.

If you achieve **Digital Distinction**, you can copy the HTML code provided to give to your developer to put on your website/blog (or you can enter the HTML yourself, if you created your own website/blog). I included this on the first page of my website/blog. I like the fact that a person can click my badge and be directed to the Online Identity Calculator to try it out for themselves.

What if you are only digitally disguised or digitally dabbling? Don't despair! Many strategies exist to build your online identity. If you are digitally disastrous, there are a couple of things you can do to try to overcome it; however, it largely depends on the website that houses the digital dirt about you. What do I mean? An example might include an unfavorable article about you in 'The New York Times.' 'The New York Times' probably will not remove the content, and they are such a high-ranking site that it will be difficult to push the information down in your Google results.

What If I Have Digital Dirt?

Digital dirt is any content that exists that is unflattering about you. The two strategies for dealing with digital dirt are to try to remove what's out there that is unflattering or develop enough content that you push the digital dirt past page three of your Google search. The following quote comes from a study done by **iProspect:**

"iProspect has trending information from previous studies, key among them is that 68 percent of search engine users click a search result within the first page of results, and a full 92 percent of search engine users click a result within the first three pages of search results. The importance of appearing high in the search results has steadily increased over time."[4]

So, what does that mean if you have digital dirt? You can utilize one of the two aforementioned strategies. As these statistics demonstrate, most people (92 percent) click a result within the first three pages of search results.

Let's look at getting rid of negative results. Many services have emerged now to help people get rid of digital dirt. There is an easy way to remove digital dirt if you created it yourself—you can simply remove or delete it. However, if you don't control the content, then you will have to make the request to the person who does control it or have a service, such as Reputation (http://www.reputation.com), to make the request for you. Sometimes this works and other times it does not.

Again, if it's a highly-regarded source like 'The Wall Street Journal,' or 'The New York Times,' or a high-ranking website, you will probably not be able to get them to remove the content. Additionally, it will not move past page three of your Google results because something like this will rank higher in the Google algorithm. The best you can do in this circumstance is to develop branded, pertinent results that hopefully show you in a different light. You might even write blog pieces about what you learned from the experience. Reach Communications (http://www.reachpersonalbranding.com) has trained people on how to implement strategies to help you with digital dirt.

Protect your brand and make sure that you are not the victim of something that goes viral. People have lost jobs and opportunities from things that are less than flattering being posted on the Internet. In the wake of video and camera phones, it is very easy

---

4. iProspect, "iProspect Blended Search Results Study (2008)," iProspect, April 2008, http://tinyurl.com/4n88ab (accessed August 26, 2009). iprospect.com/about/researchstudy_2008_blendedsearchresults.htm.

for something to be uploaded to the web and spread virally. When this happens, it becomes difficult to remove the content because it's been re-posted by other people.

On this part of your job search marketing plan, let's benchmark where you fell on the Online ID Calculator (you can go back as you start building your results to check your progress):

Date: _____

Score: _____

Personal Brand

Before you start building your brand and content online, you first need to know your personal brand. Personal brand? What's a personal brand, you ask? As William Arruda, President of Reach Communications, says:

> Your Personal Brand is nothing more than your unique promise of value.[5]

Essentially, you want to see how you are different from everyone else who has the same job title as you. What can you UNIQUELY deliver and how are you innovative as compared to your peers? The personal branding process delves into introspective work that involves discovering not only what you think of yourself, but how others view you.

How do you discover how other people see you? Reach Communications has developed a REACH 360 Personal Brand assessment that is a web-based tool that ensures the confidentiality of the people who answer the survey about you. Why is that important? You want to make sure that people feel that they can give you honest feedback—it's what will help you see how those around you view you. You can take a free, public version (does not aggregate the results—you can pay an

---

5. William Arruda and Kirsten Dixson, *Career Distinction: Stand Out by Building Your Brand* (Hoboken: John Wiley & Sons, 2007).

additional fee to upgrade to receive a twenty-page report of your results provided you have at least ten people respond to the survey). The free fifteen-day version is available at http://www.reachcc.com/360v5register.

I know what you are thinking—why does this matter? I just want to build some results online so that when an employer, recruiter, or hiring manager is researching me, I show up on Google. The problem with not taking the time to go through the personal branding process BEFORE you start building Google results is that your Google results will not tell people the consistent story of how you are UNIQUE. Companies want to know how you are different and how your special abilities will support the corporate brand.

The personal branding process is a book within itself and I'd highly recommend the book, 'Career Distinction: Stand Out by Building Your Brand' by William Arruda and Kirsten Dixson. They have also developed the Reach Branding Club (http://www.reachbrandingclub.com) for a yearly membership fee that gives you access to on-demand video modules and a workbook to help you work through the personal branding process. Additionally, the Reach Personal Branding website lists the strategists they have certified to coach people through the personal branding process (http://www.reachpersonalbranding.com).

The personal branding process helped me to see that other people view me as forward thinking, innovative, and the go-to person for technology. After I went through the process, I realized I could combine my love of technology into an occupation as a career consultant that separated me from my peers. I can offer people not only the strategies for job searching, but also help them implement social media roadmap strategies, build web-sites/blogs, etc. to aid them in a job search or for people just starting in business. I found my "sweet spot" and love what I do!

Another tool I recommend to people is the 'StrengthsFinder 2.0' evaluation by Tom Rath. You can purchase the book and you will find a code in the book to use at the website to take the assess-ment. You will find out your top 5 strengths. Most people hate having to answer the question, "What are your strengths?" (probably as much as the question, "What are your weaknesses?"). By taking this assessment, you will be able to find out your strong points.

Here, we are going to list your Top 5 Brand Attributes, Team Role, and Leadership Role from the Reach 360 Personal Brand Assessment as well as the Top 5 Strengths according to StrengthsFinder:

Top 5 Brand Attributes:

1. _____

2. _____

3. _____

4. _____

5. _____

Team Role

_____

Leadership Role

_____

Were you surprised by any of the results? If so, explain below:

_____

_____

_____

Were your results consistent with the brand you want to express? If no, what are some action items you can do to more clearly express your thought leadership and expertise?

_____

_____

_____

_____

_____

Top 5 Strengths (from StrengthsFinder, if you take this assessment)

1. _____

2. _____

3. _____

4. _____

5. _____

You now have some information to formulate your elevator pitch—that is a quick way for you to introduce who you are, what you do, and what makes you unique. One of my colleagues, Susan Chritton of Pathways, found a great resource to keep your elevator pitch (how you introduce yourself in networking—online and in person) short and simple. You can visit the website at http://www.15secondpitch.com/new/. The feature I appreciate is they only give you 500 characters total to write your pitch. The Pitch Wizard asks you a series of questions to help you formulate your statement.

Copy your elevator pitch in the space below:

_____

_____

_____

_____

_____

You can save your elevator pitch in JibberJobber. Go to "Interview Prep" on the menu and select "Add" under "30 seconds." Type your elevator pitch here and save.

4 Building Your Visibility on Google

Now that I understand how I want other people to see me, I have been able to formulate a clear strategy on how to build my Google results so that when someone googles me, they know what I do and how I'm different from other career consultants.

When I first did my own Online Identity Calculator, I was Digitally Disguised. I had one Google result—that I was on my grandmother's prayer list at her church while my former husband was overseas. They apparently publish their prayer list on the Internet and it showed up as my one and only result.

The good news about being digitally disguised or digitally dabbling is that you don't have much out there in cyberspace, so building on-brand, relevant Google results will not be that hard.

First Know Your Target Audience

When I work with people, I always encourage them to come up with a list of targeted companies where they would like to work. You want to research these companies to find out what challenges they face, who their competitors are, and most importantly, whether or not they are viable in the current marketplace. Why? You want to target your communications and build Google results on platforms where they participate.

We are going to focus on three major social networking sites in this book that JobVite's 2011 Social Recruitment survey ranks as the top three sites where companies and recruiters find and attract talent. However, realize that there are thousands of social networking sites, some of which are industry specific. You will want to do research to find out the sites where your target audience is active. For example, Flickr is an online community for photographers; Medical Mingle is a social network for the medical field; Active Rain is a professional networking site for realtors; and Ning is actually an online service that allows you to create, customize, and share a social network.

Increasing Your Visibility Online

The following five social media and Web 2.0 strategies that I will present are what might comprise part of your communications plan for your job search marketing. Prior to developing your communications plan (also part of the personal branding process), you need to find out how to reach your target audience. Find out what they read, what websites might they visit, what interests them, and so on.

The five strategies include:

1. Writing articles and/or white papers and having them published online
2. Blogging
3. Commenting on other blogs that are relevant to your thought leadership and are classified as high-ranking blogs
4. Professional profiles on social/professional networks
5. Video social networking platforms (such as YouTube, UStream.tv, Vimeo, and videoBIO)

You may choose to implement all five strategies (and of course, more strategies exist than just this list) or pick and choose which works best in your communications wheel to reach your target audience.

How many of these strategies would you wish to include in your communications plan?

_____

List the ones you might consider:

_____

_____

_____

_____

Who is your target audience?

_____

_____

_____

Which social networking platforms provided your target audience?

_____

_____

_____

_____

_____

Research Resources

Again, you want to develop a list of targeted companies where you'd like to work. In this section, I'm going to provide you with some research tools to use to help you formulate your list.

Industry Trends: You want to see the trends in different industries to know which industries might be a good match for your skills and abilities. You can go to http://www.simplyhired.com/a/jobtrends/home to locate trends within different industries. For example, when I searched on "Teacher" trends, I found that since August 2010, the following has occurred: Math Teacher jobs increased 114%; English Teacher jobs did not change; and Music Teacher jobs increased 15%.

Is your industry experiencing growth?

_____

If no, are there other industries in growth mode that are interesting to you (leveraging your skills and abilities)?

_____

If so, list those industries:

_____

_____

_____

_____

_____

ZoomInfo: Another great research resource is ZoomInfo (http://www.zoominfo.com). You can search for companies by using keywords related to a company's location (e.g., proximity to you), company size (e.g., amount of revenues, number of employees), and other related information.

Click the tab for company search and there will be a column on the left-hand side that gives you search parameters, such as "Company Name / URL / Ticker," "Industry Keywords," and "City / State / ZIP."

I ran a search on the keywords "manufacturing" and "South Carolina" and received 572 results. When I clicked a company, I got very detailed information that would be useful in research and in creating a list of targeted companies where I might want to work. Not only did I get a description, but I also got information about their revenues, number of employees, their website statistics, links to news articles, and top competitors. Did I mention that I got this information for free?

TIP: Run a search on your own name on ZoomInfo and make sure, if you show up in their search results, that the information contained is accurate. If you are not listed, create a listing for yourself. Recruiters use ZoomInfo as a resource to source candidates.

Jigsaw.com: This is another resource for company research. You can run searches similar to the one I discussed and receive a free company mini-profile. Just click "Advanced Search" and select "Find Companies." For this search, I selected Atlanta, GA and the industry of "Computers & Electronics" with the sub-industry of "IT Network Support and Services." My search returned 231 companies.

Lastly, **Google** can provide a wealth of information. Play around with some search terms to find companies to target. For example, I googled "growing companies in pharmaceutical sales 2012" and returned not only resources listing these types of companies, but also job postings.

For this section, answer the following questions:

Industry/industries where you want to work?

_____

_____

_____

What are the trends in the industry/industries you selected?

_____

_____

_____

List the companies you want to target (use separate sheets of paper) after you ran some searches.

_____

_____

_____

_____

_____

_____

_____

Are you listed on ZoomInfo? If not, have you added your profile?

_____

Note the names of the people within the company as well as your other research (i.e., recent articles, press releases, revenues, top competitors, etc.) on separate sheets of paper or within JibberJobber.com. We'll use the company names and people's names later in the social media section of the book.

**JibberJobber** provides an excellent place for you to store your research. Mouse over the tab that says "Companies" and select "Add a Company," "Target Companies," and/or "Recruiters" to store the relevant research you have found on these subjects.

Executing Google Visibility Strategies

Hopefully at this point, you've gone through the personal branding process and you know the following:

- Your personal brand

- Your elevator pitch

- Your goals, visions, aims, and so on

- Define your target audience and where and how to communicate with them

- Understand how it is you want to portray your personal brand in all communications that you do online

Strategy #1: Writing Articles and/or White Papers and Having Them Published Online

You can google "article banks" or even industry-specific journals to find out places to submit your articles. I recommend that you submit to places that will reach your target audience and are niche specific. I have submitted my articles to Ezinearticles.com and my results are usually on the first three pages of my Google results. I write articles for 'YOUnique'—a personal branding newsletter with subscribers who are very much interested in the personal branding process—therefore, I'm writing on a platform that reaches my target audience. Each article I write creates a Google result.

Not only does writing articles demonstrate your knowledge and expertise on certain subjects, but also gives you "pre-qualified" leads. I have had people contact me after reading my article and they were already interested in working with me. I did no cold-calling or advertising directly to these people, but I was able to give them a warm lead about who I am, how I work, and what I know. I have mapped this into my communications plan to write two articles per month—I've already seen the benefits of having just a few articles on the Internet.

Another idea is to be interviewed for an article. Not sure how to go about being interviewed by a reporter? Peter Shankman (you can follow him on Twitter at http://twitter.com/skydiver) has a website called "HARO—Help a Reporter Out" at http://www.helpareporter.com. You can subscribe to his email list and each day, you'll receive up to three emails (each has approximately 15–30 queries). If you see a query you might answer, he provides you information on how to contact the reporter and the best practices to use when responding to a request. I subscribe to his emails and have seen reporter requests looking for people in a job search. You can answer those types of queries or queries dealing with your expertise.

If you plan to use this strategy, execute some searches on trade journals, magazines, and other publications that your target audience may be reading. What are your search results?

_____

_____

_____

Strategy #2: Blogging

For some people, the concept of blogging seems overwhelming, but I can say that blogging regularly has really helped me in my own professional life. Not only do I blog on my website, but I have guest privileges on http://www.thepersonalbrandingblog.com. I cross-post my blog pieces to the other blogs where I have guest privileges and that strategy gives me additional Google results. I will point out, though, that when you cross-post a blog (repurpose material), you do want to make some modifications/changes to the content. If you don't, Google will count it as a strike.

Again, with blogging, you want to promote your personal brand, thought leadership, and expertise. If I visit your website, will I be able to read your blog posts, know who you are, and your personal brand?

Where do you set up a blogging platform? Many exist, but here are the top four most commonly used (at this writing):

WordPress.com is free and is hosted on their domain. The drawback is there is no customization—you can use it almost like MS Word—it's very much what you see is what you get. So, if you are not comfortable with HTML coding (as is required to customize with WordPress.org), this is a good platform. If you want to customize your HTML code, you'll be very limited here with the customization options (themes, plug-ins, and so on). It makes it a little harder to integrate social media for those reasons.

WordPress.org is the self-hosted version of WordPress—it is free, but you will install it on your own domain (i.e., GoDaddy, BlueHost, Dream-Host, MediaTemple, JustHost, Laughing Squid, or any other). Because it is on your domain, you control your content and your search engine optimization (SEO).

At this writing, WordPress.org has 36 pages of free themes built inside the control panel, but if you want a premium theme or a theme developed by a certain designer, you will have to upload it to the administrative panel. It is open source (created to be used by the general public and free to modify), so there are a wide variety of themes and plug-ins available to increase your site's functionality, look, and feel. It's a great base for social media because of all the plug-ins that are available for use with it.

TypePad.com has several apps and widgets you can integrate into the site. It's pretty straightforward and you can customize your banner to upload on this site. I have hosted my blog and website here and really like how easy it is to use. You do pay a monthly fee for the service, but this gives you access to customer service. They have a tremendous knowledge base where you can search and find the answer to almost any question you have about how to do something.

You can point a domain name to the site (I recommend using GoDaddy for this as it is really easy to do—the knowledge base has step-by-step directions/screenshots on how to do it). I used to have my own name http://www.kristenjacoway.com and http://careerdesigncoach.com pointing to my TypePad website/blog when I hosted my site there. **As part of developing online identity and thought leadership, it is recommmended to buy your own name as the domain name. When purchasing, try to get a .com name.** TypePad offers service at different levels depending on what you want to do, and ranges from beginner all the way up to someone who is familiar with coding and CSS (Cascading Style Sheets).

Blogger.com, owned by Google, is free, and is hosted on their domain. It is a basic blogging platform and no customization of code is required for this site, so you will not be able to modify the look and feel of the blog.

Tips for Starting and Maintaining Your Blog

You know you want to blog, but you are not sure how to start or maintain your blog. Why even start a blog? If you are serious about career management, one of the best ways to demonstrate your expertise and market your strengths is through blogging. How do you get started, though?

- Publish on a consistent basis—meaning, pick the days of the week when you plan to post. As you develop a readership, people will come to depend that they can visit your blog/website on certain days and see new content. Even if you can only commit to blogging twice a month, choose dates like the 15th and the 30th of the month. You might add in your blog post—"In the next post, coming up on the 30th of this month, we will look at...."

- Pick topics that are near and dear to you and really leverage your knowledge/expertise for which you want to be known. I have done series on blogging, social media platforms, and the like. I find that writing a series helps me to generate content quickly as I can divide it across several posts.

- Look at trending topics on Twitter, headlining in newspapers, in *People* magazine, and other material to get some ideas on how to pull relevant and popular topics into your blog. For example, I read many blog posts about the personal brand of Michael Jackson in the weeks following his death. People are searching on those keywords, so from time to time, this is a strategy that will help your blog get noticed.

- Speaking of keywords, you can install the free SEO Blogger (http://labs.wordtracker.com/seo-blogger/) on your Firefox browser to optimize your blog posts as you write. You can type in a word and it will generate the most popular keywords people are searching for that relate to that word.

- Read through your email answers and answers to people on Twitter and LinkedIn—what questions are people asking frequently? Write a blog post that answers the most frequently asked questions.

- Write quick tips or record a quick "How To" video, upload to YouTube, and embed the HTML in your blog post (see "How to Insert Video into Your Blog" at: http://www.youtube.com/watch?v=kuVqFyEtEFM). I did a series on online identity quick tips that were no more than two sentences long.

- You can also link people to another blog. Give a quick summary and provide the link to the blog post you read—it's a great way to join the blogging community by promoting other people's blogs.

- Just do it! I remember when I first heard the term "blogging." I had no idea what blogging was and why I needed to blog. Now that I've been blogging for four years, I'm glad I took the leap of faith and jumped in with both feet. It's fun to see those original blog posts and see how much I've learned in the last few years.

A great resource in the area of blogging is Darren Rowse at http://www.problogger.net. He has an eBook, '31 Days to a Better Blog,' that literally takes you day by day to writing and maintaining a great blog site.

If you are going to use this strategy, brainstorm some topics for at least ten blog posts (if you post just twice per month, this will give you nearly a half of a year's worth of blog posts that you can schedule).

1. _____
2. _____
3. _____
4. _____
5. _____
6. _____
7. _____
8. _____
9. _____
10. _____

If you are going to blog, which blogging platform will work best for you?

Do you have your own name registered as a domain name?

Claim your blog at Technorati (http://www.technorati.com). You will have to register for an account and go through the steps to claim your blog.

Strategies to Promote Your Blog

When I first started blogging, I felt like I was blogging to a blank wall. I wondered when I would get a comment and get to engage with others on my blog. So many tools exist now that really help to promote your blog on other social media platforms, quickly and for free. Let's look at a few ways you can use to promote your blog:

- You can use a service called Twitterfeed (http://twitterfeed.com) to automatically update your Twitter status when you write a blog post.

- On Facebook, you can search for the RSS Graffiti app on the Facebook Search box. By allowing this app to work and going through the steps of verifying ownership of this blog, your blog will automatically post to your Facebook personal and/or business page. The feature I like is that if you insert a picture into your blog post (I recommend doing this to attract readers' attention), it will pull this picture next to the status update.

- On LinkedIn, go to their applications and select the WordPress or TypePad application (depending on which blogging platform you use). You will complete the information and be able to import your blog to LinkedIn. Here, people will only see a "teaser" of what's in your blog post. They will have to click the hyperlinked title to read the entire blog post on your website.

- This may seem simple, but make sure to include your website/blog URL in your email signature. I've looked at my analytics to see from where my traffic comes—a good portion comes through people clicking my URL in my emails.

Strategy #3: Commenting on Other Blogs

Building relationships in the blogging community can be achieved by commenting on other people's blog posts in such a way that it adds value to what is written. Technorati (http://www.technorati.com) and AllTop (http://www.alltop.com) provide a search engine for you to find blogs in your niche area. Look at the blog's authority ranking to see which blogs are highly ranked. Again, you want to post comments where your target audience will see you. Not only are you building relationships, but your comments become part of your Google results and it's easy to do! As a blogger, if someone comments on my post, I take the time to look at their website and learn more about them.

One resource that I recommend is to get a **Gravatar** (http://www.gravatar.com). Gravatar simply stands for a Globally Recognized Avatar and is an image (your headshot that you upload) that will follow you from site to site and appears beside your name when you post. It's free and all that is required is your email address. It helps you to expand your brand's recognition as people start to associate your face with your name.

If you plan to implement this strategy, list the top-ranking blogs in your niche that you found on Technorati or AllTop. Additionally, subscribe to the blog either via email or the RSS feed (stands for Real Simple Syndication). You basically will have that blog's feed bookmarked and you can check to see when there are new posts.

List five relevant, high-ranking blogs on which to comment.

1. _____

2. _____

3. _____

4. _____

5. _____

Do you have a Gravatar yet? _____

Strategy #4: Professional Profiles on Social Networking Sites

Another great opportunity for building Google visibility is creating on-brand and detailed profiles on professional networking websites. Again, measure where you can reach your target audience. Many exist, and some of the most popular include LinkedIn, Ziggs, Spoke, Ecademy, and Facebook. You can also create a profile on Google+ that is a new social networking platform that launched in the summer of 2011 (http://www.google.com/profiles). I always tell people to choose two to three platforms where they can reach their target audience and be active on those platforms. If you sign up for multiple professional networking sites, you will not be able to give them good focus.

Look at some of these professional networking sites and see which ones would work best in your communications plan. Which ones are you considering?

_____

_____

_____

Strategy #5: Video Social Networking Platforms

YouTube and other online video social networking platforms are becoming emerging trends for showing thought leadership. Some people have their own YouTube (http://www.youtube.com) channel and UStream channel (http://www.ustream.tv). People can subscribe to your channel and will be notified when you post new content. You can even brand your channel page with your brand identity fonts, colors, images, etc. Erin Blaskie does a free Live Q & A session every week on UStream. She has built a following using this strategy and people feel like they have really connected with her through this medium. Again, it's the know, like, and trust factor.

How can you use these media as part of your communications strategy? I post several "How To" videos on YouTube. I do short screen recordings with a software package such as Camstasia Studio (http://www.techsmith.com) or with the Jing Project (download for free at http://www.jingproject.com —you are limited to 5 minutes, though). I've edited my channel page to include my website, so people can learn more about me there and contact me. Again, using YouTube allows me to show people a new dimension of what I can do, how I speak, present, and so on. You could also upload PowerPoint presentations to YouTube (or another similar service called SlideShare—http://www.slideshare.net).

I have seen a handful of clients who were asked to submit a YouTube video as part of the interview process. Additionally, I have read of others being asked to do the same, so I felt that this is becoming a relevant topic to include in this book.

Recommendations and Resources for Creating Compelling Videos

I had the opportunity to interview Erin Blaskie (http://www.erinblaskieinc.com) of BSETC about YouTube.[6] We discussed ideas for content development, promoting and driving traffic to the video, and tips for producing good videos.

Often, when people are asked to develop a YouTube video, the first question is usually centered on what kind of video to produce. Erin gave the following suggestions:

- "How to" videos or live demonstrations (using charts and other visual aids) that promote your thought leadership.

---

6. Erin Blaskie, Owner of Business Services, ETC. and The VA Coach, interviewed by Kristen Jacoway (July 31, 2009).

- A short (two minutes or less) tip video that shows your expertise and/or helps to solve a problem.

- Interviewing another business person about trending topics in your field.

- Conducting a live Question & Answer series.

We then discussed strategies to drive traffic to your video. Videos can provide a different dimension that your résumé alone cannot demonstrate—it shows your personality, how you present material, and other such aspects. Therefore, YouTube (and other video social networking platforms) is another resource in building your visibility online. Uploading "How To" videos or tip videos has created new Google results for my name. Erin suggested the following strategies for driving traffic to your video:

- Promote your video on other social media platforms. Update your status by posting the URL of the video on Twitter, Facebook, LinkedIn, or other social networks where you belong.

- Improve your SEO by including the keywords in your title that people might be searching for to solve a problem.

- She highly recommends uploading the video to YouTube. According to the Press Release facts on the YouTube website, there are more than 3 billion views per day and that 60 hours of video are being uploaded every minute to the website.[7]

- You can also embed your video HTML code into your blog post to show your video. You can view a tutorial at: http://www.youtube.com/watch?v=kuVqFyEtEFM.

- In the description box describing your video, Erin recommends that you lead the description with your website URL address (again, this can be a link to your website/web portfolio/blog, LinkedIn profile, Twitter account, etc.). Make sure to start the link with http:// so that it becomes a clickable link.

---

7. YouTube, "YouTube Fact Sheet," YouTube,
   http://www.youtube.com/t/press, (accessed April 20, 2012).

Lastly, we talked about ways to produce a good quality video. Erin shared the following tips and resources:

- She recommends a Flip camera—she uses the Flip Mini HD camera. You can either have someone hold it or place it on a tripod. You can also use a built-in camera on your computer.

- If you are doing screen recordings of your computer, I recommend Camstasia Studio for lengthy projects, and Jing Project for less than five minute projects. Both Camstasia Studio and Jing Project work on Windows and Mac operating systems.

- Erin suggested that if you are recording yourself, you need to make sure you are in a well-lit room and that the lighting is not casting a shadow on your face. Do a trial take first and review to ensure that the lighting is adequate.

- She shared a great tip for doing a presentation—buy a large Post-It Flip Chart that you can tape on a wall directly in front of you that lists the main points of your presentation. The key is not to read the entire presentation, but to know the material well enough so that the chart just facilitates what you are going to say.

- She recommends editing your videos with either iMovie with a Mac or with Windows MovieMaker.

Videos are a great way to promote your thought leadership and expertise, so you may consider this as one of your communication strategies with your target audience. The tips and resources Erin Blaskie provided should serve as a great way for you to get started and delve into the video social networking platform.

videoBIO

An emerging trend is video biographies for web for everyone from job seekers to executives to small business owners. videoBIO (http://www.videobio.com) is based in Toronto and New York with plans to rollout videoBIO studios in major cities across North America over the next year. The videoBIO process starts with a script. They will have you complete a "Know Your Character" quick online assessment to measure five areas: personality, motivational style, relational style, communication style, and leadership style. The results become a basis for formulating your script outline, which also takes into account your target market, overall key messages and highlights from other supporting documents (such as résumé, cover letter, and career highlights).

The end product is a three-minute video biography edited from a thirty-minute on-camera interview. You can preview some of the videoBIOs that have been produced for customers at http://videobio.com/page/products/. Each videoBIO customer will have their video posted to a custom http://videoBIO.com web profile page that includes embedded code allowing you to easily post and share your videoBIO on social networking platforms such as Facebook, LinkedIn, YouTube, and Plaxo, and as a link, in your email signature.

videoBIO is an excellent way to managing your professional reputation online and convey your personal brand story in a consistent, personalized way. It can help you to stand apart from your competition. It's also an innovative way to reach potential employers as a career marketing tool in communicating your unique value.

What's Your Google Quotient Now?

You have many options available to you to increase your visibility on Google. Find which ones are right for you and then deliver them to outlets to reach your target audience. Stay true to who you are and how you want others to see you. Be authentic and be yourself! Go back and check your online identity results throughout the process. Set a Google Alert (http://www.google.com/alerts) on your name by putting your name in quotation marks ("Kristen Jacoway") to get more relevant results. Benchmark your results today and then, after implementing these strategies, see how you progress on the quadrant of Digital Distinction. Remember, Google's algorithm changes periodically. You will want to check your results regularly so you can maintain Digital Distinction once you've achieved it.

Which day of the week will you google your name?

_____

Let's chart your progress during the next several weeks (you don't need to check your online identity calculator score every week—just do so periodically):

Date	Number of Relevant Google Results	Online ID Score

5 Career Marketing Material

Résumés

My family has recently moved and I have been amazed at how much stuff there is to unpack. I question why we still have things that we have been moving throughout the Southeast U.S.

It brings me to a point I see with résumés—either people don't have enough information or it's what I like to term as a "data dump" where they've included everything they've done from 30 years ago, have it set to an 8 point font, and the margins are so small that it's out of print range. I do encourage people to keep a journal of their achievements (in a Challenge, Action, and Result format), but don't advise that every achievement be placed on a résumé if it's not applicable to the position for which they are applying. Most agree that listing your top 3–7 achievements per position is sufficient. If you list more than that, you run the risk of bogging your reader down with too many details. Most people won't take that kind of time to read all the details of your résumé. My best analogy? Think of your résumé as you would your suitcase—pack only what you need for the next journey.

The general rule of thumb is to only go back in your work history for 10–15 years. You can truncate the remainder in a section called "Additional Work Experience."

Example of one way to format the "Additional Work Experience" section:

ABC COMPANY • Santa Clara, CA
Vice President

One way to "customize" your résumé is to review your achievements against the requirements for the position. Then, you may choose to cut, add, or replace data to highlight how your achievements will help that particular employer.

The Components of a Résumé

I'm going to focus on each part of the résumé in this section and will note where you may want to customize certain areas when applying for positions.

1. **Contact Information:** Debate has centered on whether or not it's necessary to include addresses under the contact section. If you are posting your résumé to a job board and not to a particular position, I feel that either a P.O. Box or just the city and state are sufficient. Additionally, I advise people to sign up for an email account that is just for your career transition at Gmail, Yahoo, or any other mail client. Using this strategy helps you to separate personal email from job searching email and facilitates you to keep track of the follow up you need to do. By the way, please just use your first name and last name for this email address for a professional appearance. You'd be surprised at how many résumés I've seen where a person has "mythreegirls@...."

2. **Profile:** On the profile you want a well-written summary of what you've done and what separates you from your peers with the same job title (your personal brand statement). Your profile should be customized to answer the question, "What's in it for me?" for the employer. Read the job posting carefully and make sure you are highlighting the skills and achievements that support the requirements for the job. Many people just send out their

résumé and do nothing to customize it. In today's marketplace, this strategy does NOT work. Why? Again, an employer is not going to take the time to "read between the lines" to see why you are the best fit. You have to make it very clear why you are the best person and the profile is an excellent place to make your case. Keep your profile to one paragraph.

Above your profile, you can put the name of the position for which you are applying. If you are uploading to a job board or sending to a recruiter, then you can put a general job title that best describes what you want to do. When we submit my former husband's résumé to a job board, we put "Manufacturing Management" as his broad term.

3. **Keyword Summary/Core Competencies:** You want a section that has keywords (no more than 9–12) that highlight your skills and abilities. Two of my favorite books on keywords are '2500 Keywords to Get You Hired' by Jay Block and 'Best Keywords for Résumés, Cover Letters, and Interviews' by Wendy Enelow. Wendy's book not only includes keywords, but also key phrases that will be helpful when writing your job description. We will discuss the importance of keywords a little later.

4. **Professional Experience:** You will want to list your positions in reverse order, starting with your most recent position. Most employers and hiring managers are only interested in the last 10–15 years of experience, as that experience is what is relevant for today's market challenges. You can truncate the remainder in "Additional Professional Experience" (see the example in the section "Résumés").

   Under the company name, you will want to describe the company. You can normally find this information in the "About" section of a company's website, ZoomInfo.com, or on Hoovers.com. If you can provide information about the company's revenues and number of employees, this is helpful information to include. Also, is it a Fortune 500 company? Think about what might matter to a potential employer. Keep your description brief. You want no more than two sentences for a company description.

5. **Job Descriptions:** Keep your job descriptions to four to six sentences. Job descriptions are another prime opportunity to customize your résumé. For example, I applied for a position where working with college students was one of the

qualifications. I had done this for seven years as a vocational counselor as one of the many parts of my position. However, I did not have this listed in my résumé. I read the job requirements and customized this area of my résumé to show my applicable experience for their top three requirements.

In your job description, ask yourself these questions:

  i. Did I manage revenues, and if yes, how much?

 ii. Did I manage budgets, and if yes, how much?

iii. Did I supervise people, and if yes, how many?

iv. What territories did I cover in this position, if any?

A great place to find additional information about tasks, knowledge, skills, and abilities for positions for which you are applying is O*Net (http://online.onetcenter.org/find). You can search on a keyword for an occupation. When I searched on "Career Counselor" I found 321 related occupations. Some titles had an "Bright Outlook" written beside them. When you click a job title, you will receive the following information: a summary; tasks; tools and technology; knowledge; skills; abilities; work activities; work context; job zone; interests; work styles; work values; related occupations; and wages.

Remember, you want to write towards the position for which you are applying and highlight the job duties and achievements that support the requirements for that position.

6. **Achievements:** I have an entire section, "Achievement Stories for Your Résumé," devoted to writing achievements, later in the book. In today's marketplace, achievements are what will distinguish your résumé. Wherever possible, quantify your achievements. Don't data dump. Listing your top three to seven achievements per position is plenty. If you have more than seven achievements for a position, read the job posting. What's important to that employer? Support the job requirements with achievements that relate to what the employer is seeking.

7. **Education:** You want to remember to spell out the name of the degree and include the abbreviation, i.e., Master of Business Administration (MBA). Sometimes, people use one or the other when setting up search parameters on résumé scanning software, so be sure you are covered either way.

Other résumé components can include Honors and Awards, Professional Development, Certifications, Publications, and so on.

NOTE: Don't use the header function for your contact information as sometimes it will not pass through a résumé scanning software program. Type it in as you would the rest of the text. You can use a footer, though (and I recommend doing this) that includes your name and the page number of the résumé.

The Importance of Keywords

In today's competitive marketplace, résumé scanning software are becoming utilized more and more as companies are seeking ways to identify top industry performers in the midst of hundreds of résumés received for a job posting. How can you make sure that your résumé is found? Keywords in a résumé are similar to search optimization strategies for websites. It is very important to include keywords in your résumé to help increase the odds of having it reviewed.

Keywords fall into several categories: hard skills, soft skills, educational background, geographic location, and many more. Hard skills are tangible duties/achievements such as P & L management, Revenue Growth, Cost Containment, and so on. Soft skills include presentation skills and team leadership. Search parameters for educational background may include not only the type of degree and major, but also the name of the university or college. Geographical location may be included in a search to identify candidates located in a certain city, state, or region.

As you write your résumé, be sure to write toward the future for the type of position for which you are seeking. Emphasize areas that directly link your skills to that type of position and de-emphasize the duties or achievements that are not related. As you read job postings for positions for which you are interested, note the keywords (noun and noun phrases) they use throughout the listing. Are those keywords on your résumé? One strategy you can use to customize your résumé for a particular position is to interweave keywords in a job posting that are applicable to your background and experience. Why is that important? If the hiring manager wrote that job posting, chances are greater that those keywords will be in the search parameters that he/she utilizes.

Let's look at a job posting I found. I've italicized some of the potential keywords on this listing:

Key Account Sales Manager – *Little Rock, AR* (geography keyword)

Organization

Consumer and Office Business

Primary Location

USA Region-United States-Arkansas-Little Rock

Job Type

Experienced

Description

We are currently seeking *Key Account Sales Manager* within ABC Company's Home Care Division.

The responsibilities of this position include, but are not limited to the following:

- Development and implementation of *strategic sales plans* into assigned XXXX and XXXX Club Departments.

- *Selling existing and new products* into additional departments within XXXX and XXXX Club.

- *Enhancement of relationships at all levels and in all departments* (Buying, Replenishment, Marketing, Store Operations, etc.) within XXXX and XXXX Club.

- Development of *forecasts* for *sales planning* and *demand planning* purposes and for the *management of trade performance budgets.*

Qualifications

Basic/Minimum Qualifications:

- *Bachelor's degree* required.

- *Five (5) or more years* of relevant sales experience.

Preferred qualifications:

- *MBA* preferred.

- Strong *analytical skills.*

- Proven ability to develop strong *customer relationships.*

- Proven record of *exceeding sales forecasts.*

- Strong proficiency with computer applications, especially *Excel* and *PowerPoint.*

- *Consumer packaged goods industry experience.*

So, in this posting, we see the following **potential** keywords:

Arkansas (geography), Key Account Sales Manager (you will want to reference this title at the top of your résumé under your contact information AND in your cover letter), strategic sales plans, sales skills (i.e., B2B, B2C, consultative selling, and/or solution-based sales techniques), forecasting, sales planning, demand planning, budget management, Bachelor's degree (BS degree—remember to use abbreviations, too!), analytical skills, account development/retention, revenue growth, Excel and PowerPoint, and consumer packaged goods industry experience.

See how you can sleuth to find potential keywords in a job posting? **Of course, you only want to interweave the keywords that are applicable to your background and experience.**

Tips for Customizing Your Résumé

Always make sure that you review the job posting and research the company prior to applying. You will find a wealth of information, including keywords, which will help you stand apart from the competition **if** you take the time to modify your résumé and cover letter for each position you apply.

Think about what matters to an employer. Very few, if any, will offer you a job based on your résumé alone. Your résumé is one small piece of the career marketing strategy that will help you secure the interview. If you have too much information, the employer is not going to take the time to read it. If you have too little, they are not going to play a guessing game to figure out if you will fit with their organization. In today's marketplace, YOU have to show them why you are the BEST fit.

Do you need to "spring clean" your résumé? I would suggest that you really consider doing it for each position for which you apply. Demonstrate your abilities/accomplishments for that PARTICULAR position and don't data dump. Remember, the first time someone reads your résumé, it is estimated that they spend six seconds looking at it. Make sure that this short time spent on your résumé highlights what you need for that position.

Resources for a Résumé

One of my favorite résumé book series is authored by Wendy Enelow and Louise Kursmark. You can find a full listing of their books at http://www.wendyenelow.com/bookstore.php. You can also search on Google to find résumé reference books to glean ideas for formatting, best practices, and other related information.

If you have your résumé professionally written (I prefer this approach because it's hard to be objective about your own background—what needs to remain and what needs to go), do your due diligence to find a certified résumé writer who can provide you with samples of résumés that they've written in your industry. Professional Association of Resume Writers, or PARW, (http://www.parw.com/home.html) maintains a database of certified professional résumé writers.

Achievement Stories for Your Résumé

How can you help your résumé stand apart from other résumés on a recruiter's or hiring manager's desk? Make sure you include your achievements! If you only list your job duties without achievements, then you are missing a critical piece in your résumé.

Your achievements are made up of four parts: the position you held, the assignment or project, what you did, and what was the result. You want to quantify your results where possible (i.e., percentage of productivity improvement, amount of savings captured, and amount of revenues generated). Sometimes you can add a compelling situation, such as a volatile recessionary period, to frame the achievement. Here's an example:

Generated $1 million in new revenues during a volatile recessionary period by developing XYZ new product and structuring a sales blitz to drive sales during the launch.

Let's break this down:

- **Generated $1 million in new revenues**—I generally like to start achievements with the result, if possible, to really highlight the outcome of the action.

- **During a volatile recessionary period**—this highlights the timing of the project and the obstacles that had to be overcome.

- **By developing XYZ product**—shows the task responsible for the outcome.

- **Structuring a sales blitz**—demonstrates the action taken to generate the result.

You'll note that my achievement takes no more than two lines to describe. The maximum number of lines is three, but it's really ideal to keep this as succinct as possible. You don't want to bog your reader with too many details.

As a vocational counselor for many years, I have seen many people not remember their achievements and who, unfortunately, never kept a record of their accomplishments. I really encourage people to keep a journal of the achievements and record when they happened. Keeping a journal of your achievements helps you to pull out relevant achievements to support the job qualifications and customize your résumé to show how you are a good fit for a position.

Write at least three to seven achievement stories for each position you've held during the last 10–15 years. Use separate sheets to complete this exercise.

Job Title: _____

Project/Assignment:

_____

_____

Situation:

_____

_____

What did you do:

_____

_____

_____

_____

What was the result:

_____

_____

Summarize in one or two sentences:

_____

_____

Job Title: _____

Project/Assignment:

_____

_____

Situation:

_____

_____

What did you do:

_____

_____

_____

_____

What was the result:

_____

_____

Summarize in one or two sentences:

_____

_____

Job Title: _____

Project/Assignment:

_____

_____

Situation:

_____

_____

What did you do:

_____

_____

_____

_____

What was the result:

_____

_____

Summarize in one or two sentences:

_____

_____

Top 5 Resume Tips

As important as it is to format your resume with an eye-catching look, it is increasingly important to make sure that your resume can pass through companies' resume scanning software. Many companies employ the use of resume scanning software because it helps them weed through candidates efficiently and quickly. You may have all of the qualifications and experience required for the position, but if your resume has some of the common mistakes people make or is missing crucial elements, then a human may never see your resume.

Here are my Top 5 recommendations to help you in crafting your resume for today's job search:

1. **Use a Standard Heading:** Your First Name, Your Last Name, Address, Phone Number and Email address. Why? Most resume scanning software programs are designed to capture the information in fields in this order. I had a client that had listed her address and contact information on the first two lines and then had her name on the third line in a large font. However, the database would generally capture this information as first name, "1234" and last name "Covington" instead of her real name.

2. **Only Add the BEST Contact Phone Number:** Many applicant-tracking programs will parse one phone number. I've seen numerous times where a candidate lists two to three phone numbers. You want to make sure you list the best way to reach you (i.e. your cell). Do NOT list your work number, though, for obvious reasons.

   Additionally, never put your contact information in a header or footer of the Word document. Resume scanning software is unable to "see" information contained in a header or footer and therefore, the information will not be parsed into the program. You may have all the qualifications they are seeking, but if the computer program did not "inhale" your contact information, they will have no way to know how to reach you for an interview.

3. **Never Include Your Photo or Personal Information:** Most people know not to include this information, but I have reviewed resumes at the C+ level where this information is included. If a Human Resource professional learns of your personal situation or sees a picture, then they could be faced with a discriminatory situation. Most hiring managers will delete the resume if it includes photo, marital status, number of children, status of your health, percentage of disability that an armed force has declared you, etc.

4. **Spell Out and Use Abbreviations for All Degrees, Certifications, Professional Memberships, and More:** For example, I have an M.S. degree in Vocational Counseling. On my resume, I say, "Master of Science (M.S. degree) in Vocational Counseling, *Auburn University.* I am also a Certified Rehabilitation Counselor, so I include the spelled out version and C.R.C. on my resume.

Why is this important? You do not know how someone might set up his or her search parameters in tracking software. They may search for the abbreviation, "PMP" but if you only have "Project Management Professional" listed on your resume, your resume may be missed.

5. **Keywords, Keywords, Keywords!** Look at the job posting and the nouns and noun phrases. If they apply to your background and experience, USE them in your resume. Search parameters are set up to look for these keywords and if they don't exist in your resume, then your resume will not be passed to the hiring manager from the software program.

All of these tips are critical components for your resume, but you also want to look at good formatting practices and readability. If you place company names in a 14-point font, then do so consistently throughout the resume. Likewise, if your job duties and achievements are typed in a 10-point font, make sure it carries through the entire resume in that same font and size.

TheLadders.com recently did an eye-tracking study on how recruiters viewed resumes. They found that recruiters spend a whopping six SECONDS reviewing an individual resume. To obtain a copy of this report and the key elements at which recruiters look, go to http://bit.ly/GHKwXh[8] to download this free report.

---

8. blog.theladders.com/ux/you-only-get-6-seconds-of-fame
-make-it-count/

Customizing Your Cover Letter for Each Company

Let's face it—people can smell a form letter a mile away. Are you sending the same cover letter to every position for which you apply? Successful job hunters realize that to set themselves apart from the competition, they need to customize their cover letter for each position. The letter should reflect research about the company. It also needs to address the person by name instead of saying "To Whom It May Concern" or "Dear Human Resources Manager." Do some research if it's a blind post and see if you can find the name on the company's website (or even call the company and ask what the name of the hiring manager is). If you can't find out this information, you might say in the first line that you did try to find out their name, but were unable to find the information since it was a blind post.

Demonstrate your knowledge about the company. Mention any recent articles or press releases you've read about them.

Review the job posting carefully. Take time to highlight their top three to five requirements for the position and how your skills and achievements fulfill those requirements. Be succinct and try to keep your cover letter to one page. In the wake of iPhones, BlackBerries, and other such devices, many people are reading these cover letters on handheld devices. Here's one way you can customize your cover letter (called a T-bar approach):

Your Requirements   **My Qualifications**

1. _____   _____

2. _____   _____

3. _____   _____

Write Thank-You Notes Within 24 Hours After an Interview

Surprisingly, not many job hunters write a thank-you note after a job interview. According to CareerBuilder.com's survey, "How to Get in the Front Door," nearly 15 percent of hiring managers say they would not hire someone who failed to send a thank-you letter after the interview. Interestingly, 32 percent say they would still consider the candidate, but would think less of him/her.[9]

Writing a thank you after an interview will definitely differentiate you from the crowd. More importantly, it demonstrates the ability to follow through and see a task to completion. This characteristic can demonstrate the kind of employee one will be to a company.

Check Your References

What I mean to say here is check your references and check *with* your references. Take this scenario (this is my own true story): I was working away one day and I received a call. The person on the other end stated that Jane Doe had put me down as a reference and that I supervised her during her internship. Well, here lies problem #1. I didn't remember this intern right away and I had no clue she was putting me down as her reference. I was a Certified Rehabilitation Counselor in my office and had a new intern every quarter from the surrounding universities and colleges during my tenure of seven years.

So, right away, I tried to place this person's face leaving an uncomfortable silence on the phone. I finally remembered her and tried to give her a nice recommendation. The lag time was pretty awkward.

---

9. Jennifer Sullivan, "Nearly 15 Percent of Hiring Managers Would Dismiss a Candidate Who Doesn't Send a Thank-You Letter, CareerBuilder.com Survey Finds," *PR Newswire*, August 16, 2005, http://tinyurl.com/ybgdlyh (accessed August 26, 2009). prnewswire.com/cgi-bin/sto-ries.pl?ACCT=104&STORY=/www/story/08-16-2005/0004089188 &EDATE=

Now, if Jane had called to give me some notice that someone might be calling me to get a recommendation, I would have been prepared. I could have pulled out her file and seen the evaluation I wrote to her college/university. Also, I probably would have quizzed her on the type of position, qualifications needed, skills required and really highlighted achievements that related to those qualifications. Of course, I would have asked those types of questions because I am a vocational counselor.

When you are planning to list someone as your reference, you want to reconnect with them either by phone or email. Ask permission to use them as a reference. Let them know the type of positions for which you are applying as well as the qualifications. Here's a suggestion: *Coach* your reference on a couple of your achievements that relate to the qualifications of the positions for which you are applying. Don't expect that they are going to remember that you saved the company money or generated $1 million in revenues from a product you developed. Remind them of those two to three achievements (succinctly) that will help show the potential employer why you are a good fit for that company.

NOTE: Do not put references on your résumé. Your references should only be provided to an employer when asked. Your reference sheet should be separate from your résumé and cover letter.

Business Cards

Business cards are becoming increasingly important for people in a job search as part of their career-marketing portfolio. Why? Having a business card to hand out at a networking event makes better sense than trying to hand out your résumé to everyone. Small and compact, it lends to an easy way for someone to follow up with you after a net-working event to obtain additional information. Am I saying you shouldn't take résumés to a networking event? No. However, not everyone appreciates having a résumé given to them. Present your business card first and then ask if they'd like a copy of your résumé. They may prefer you to email your résumé later because they might have a drink in one hand and a dinner plate in the other hand.

What might you include on your business card? Of course, the obvious—your name and contact information (email and/or phone number). On the back, I'd include one sentence that sums your elevator pitch and shows your personal brand.

You can design your own business card in Microsoft Word or Photoshop using the template set-up instructions from the printing supplies. You also could upload your business card or design it on an online platform such as Vista Print (http://www.vistaprint.com) or Moo (http://us.moo.com/en/). You might also want to build a business card online. One resource I found and like is Workface (http://www.workface.com)—formerly known as BusinessCard2. The bonus? Your business card will also show up on a Google search on your name. Additionally, Workface allows you to connect with your Twitter, LinkedIn, Pinterest, and Facebook accounts directly from your card. You can also list any relevant experience and credentials for the type of position you are seeking.

6 Using LinkedIn, Twitter, Facebook, and Pinterest

A recent study by Jobvite 2011 Social Recruitment Survey showed that 89 percent of companies plan to use social networks to source candidates this year. Among those using social network sites for recruiting, LinkedIn is now used by 87 percent of respondents. Facebook use is now at 55 percent in 2011. Twitter ranks third with 47 percent of recruiters using the tool to source candidates.[10] So, let's take a look at the top three sites that companies and recruiters are using to find and attract talent.

Getting Started on LinkedIn

LinkedIn, a powerful professional networking site, was launched in May 2003 and has grown to include 150 million members as of February 2012.[11] The founder is Reid Hoffman, who was previously the executive vice president at

---

10. Jobvite, "2011 Social Recruitment Survey Results," Jobvite, http://bit.ly/9Kz1qg (accessed April 24, 2012).
recruiting.jobvite.com/resources/social-recruit-ing-survey.php
11. LinkedIn, "About Us," LinkedIn, http://press.linkedin.com/about (accessed April 23, 2012).

PayPal.[12] The premise of the degrees of connection is that everyone is connected by six degrees or less. Presently I have 863 connections. My total network is 15,336,612+!

Optimized LinkedIn Profile

After you sign up for your free account with http://www.linkedin.com LinkedIn (yes, there are upgrades for a monthly charge—you can look at the plans to see which will work best for your needs, although the free account has always done what I needed to date), you will want to focus on your profile section. I'm going to walk you through this as I'm often amazed at how many people only put in their name, location, and Current Position.

Profile

On your home page, highlight the tab "**Profile**" and select "**Edit Profile**." In my profile, I have a choice to either let my full name be shown or my first name with last name initial (i.e. Kristen J.). I choose for my full name as it helps to build my online identity and gives me a Google result on my name.

Your Professional Headline

Next, you will want to fill out the "**Professional Headline**." Think in terms of keywords that someone may be using (i.e. recruiter) to find a person with your skills and expertise. Anytime you want to change one of these areas on the profile section, you'll just click the "edit" link. It's recommended that you put industry information as well as geographic location (remember recruiters and employers do "geotargeted" searches to identify talent for vacancies) to improve your chances of being found.

---

12. LinkedIn, "Management," LinkedIn,
    http://press.linkedin.com/management (accessed April 29, 2012).

Experience

In your **Current Position**, you list what it is that you do. Again, think about keywords people will use to search in this area. I'm also a big advocate of using *both the title and acronym* on all areas of your profile. For example, if you are a Chief Financial Officer, type that and "CFO." If you graduated with an MBA, type that **and** Master of Business Administration. People sometimes search on acronyms, so be sure you include all that are applicable to you.

My top advice? Do keyword research for your industry—are any of these industry keywords applicable to your experience and training? Someone in the Marketing industry might find keywords such as social media, integrated communications platforms, brand strategy, budget administration, event management, Pay-per-click (PPC) advertising, and more. Make sure your profile contains keywords in a readable format. Keyword density can be helpful, but not if it takes away from the readability.

Your Brand Story

The **Summary** section lets you deliver your brand story or your unique value proposition. Many people leave this area blank (you get ~2,000 characters to tell your story).

Work Experience

The **Experience** section lets you edit information about the current company where you are employed. Some people copy and paste information from their resume. I did more of a description here and then copied from my resume for my past positions.

Website

In the **Website** section, there is a little trick to getting it to display a custom title instead of saying "My Website and Blog." You will want to select the **"Other"** button as this lets you customize this section. So, I selected "**Other**" and typed, *"Facebook Fan Page"* and "**Other**" and *"Career Design Coach."* It lets people know the URL of where you are taking them.

Linking Twitter to LinkedIn

You can now add your Twitter URL on Twitter. You will click "**Add another Twitter account**" and allow LinkedIn to access your Twitter account by clicking, *"Authorize app."* Check the next three boxes. Displaying your Twitter account on your LinkedIn profile will allow your LinkedIn connections to connect easily with you on Twitter. By checking the next box, you can update your LinkedIn status on Twitter by adding the hashtag, "#li." When you check the final box, it will pull a picture and more rich data when you share a link on Twitter and LinkedIn.

Claim Your Vanity LinkedIn URL to Build Google Results

One of the easiest areas to brand yourself online is called the **Public Profile** and it's one that many people neglect. Normally, the default will show http://www.LinkedIn.com/in/abdec1234abs. You can click edit and replace the string of letters and numbers with your first and last name. By doing so, you create a new on-brand, relevant Google result on your name.

Skills and Expertise - beta: The Skills and Expertise feature launched in February 2011. On your profile page, you can click the tab at the top called, **"More"** and from the drop down box, select **"Skills."**

The Skills feature is still in beta, but already offers some great features for someone in a job search. I can enter my skills in the **"Search Skills & Expertise"** box and select the keyword that matches it. I can then **"Add Skill"** to my profile by clicking the box and can see, at a glance, the trends in this skill set. As you can see, while you type, LinkedIn populates the most popular search terms. If applicable, try to use one of the populated search terms, as it will facilitate **optimizing your profile**.

For example, I searched "Resume Writing" and found that this professional training and coaching industry is experiencing a 7% year over year growth. If this wasn't on my profile, I would be given the option to *list it on my profile.*

In the right-hand sidebar, I can find potential job openings in my industry. I can also discover related companies and begin to follow those companies from this page. In the middle column, you will find like-minded professionals with whom you can connect as well as networking groups that you can join.

Connecting on LinkedIn

LinkedIn has suggested that getting at least 65 connections will give you sufficient reach to do searches and find what you need.[13] People's policies on LinkedIn go from one side to the other. Some feel that they must meet you in person and break bread at the dinner table before you connect, while others are more open with their policy and accept invitations from everyone. A word of caution, though—you never know people's policy on how they will connect, so it is wise to really customize the invitation. You need to let the person know:

1. Who you are
2. How you know them
3. Why you want to connect

I received an invitation the other day from someone I didn't know, but immediately connected with this person because the person took the time to address those elements in the note to me. The note said, "Hi, I've been in the Reach master program and I'd like to add you to my professional network on LinkedIn. I visited your website http://www.careerdesigncoach.com and I like it a lot!"

So, why is this important? Because if five people click the button, "I don't know (your name)," then you start losing invitation privileges.[14]

How do you find people to connect with on LinkedIn? You can export your email address book if you have a supported platform (i.e., Gmail, Yahoo, etc.) to LinkedIn to find out if anyone you know is on LinkedIn.

---

13. Jason Alba, "Social Media Success Summit," May 2009.
14. Jason Alba, *I'm on LinkedIn—Now What??? Second Edition* (Cupertino: Happy About, 2008).

This is probably one of the best ways to find connections. I don't have one of the supported email accounts, so I exported my email list into an Excel file and uploaded the CSV file to LinkedIn.

I have been asked many times if you can disconnect from a LinkedIn contact without them receiving a notice that you disconnected. At this writing, the answer is, *yes*.[15]

Groups on LinkedIn and Networking Opportunities

You have the ability to search for groups on LinkedIn. Groups can provide an excellent way to network with professionals and thought leaders in your field. Go to the toolbar and click "Groups" and select "Groups Directory" to search for industry-specific groups. I searched on the term "Finance" and generated 11,450 groups on LinkedIn. I narrowed my search by typing "Finance and Virginia" and received 14 results. In your career transition, networking is one of the most important strategies in your job search.

Group involvement on LinkedIn is a terrific way to network, let others know you are in a job search, and show your thought leadership by answering questions that other group members pose.

Applications within LinkedIn

With your new, stellar LinkedIn profile, you will want to add apps to showcase your expertise. Used strategically, adding apps contributes to the functionality and depth of your profile. Only add apps that facilitate personal branding efforts; otherwise, your profile will appear unfocused.

---

15. LinkedIn Customer Service Center, "Removing a Connection," LinkedIn, http://tinyurl.com/ykl355t (accessed April 23, 2012). linkedin.custhelp.com/cgi-bin/linkedin.cfg/php/enduser/std_adp.php?p_faqid=49&p_created=1204033807&p_sid=fxkER-mGj&p_accessibility=0&p_redirect=&p_lva=&p_sp=cF9zcmNoPSZwX 3NvcnRfYnk9JnBfZ3JpZHNvcnQ9JnBfcm93X2NudD02NDAsNjQwJnB fcHJvZHM9JnBfY2F0cz0mcF9w

Blog Link or WordPress Application

My first favorite app is the **"Blog Link"** or **"Wordpress"** if you are blogging in your area of thought leadership. This app allows your blog to automatically feed into your LinkedIn profile. The feature I appreciate is that it gives a teaser to your blog post; however, for a person to read the entire post, they have to click the title to continue reading it on your blog thus driving traffic to your website.

One piece of advice: If your blog is about your cooking passion and you are trying to build your brand as an IT expert, then feeding your cooking blog into your LinkedIn profile will confuse the brand you are trying to build.

SlideShare Application

My second favorite app is **"SlideShare."** I use it to showcase video presentations I've done. I also know a number of people who have had a videoBIO. Utilizing videos in brand-building is a cutting-edge technique not widely done at this time, so it can really set you apart from your competition.

If you want to add other applications to your LinkedIn profile, sign in to your LinkedIn account. On the toolbar, select **"More"** and either select **"Applications"** or **"Get More Applications."** At this writing, there are *15 apps available*, including Reading List by Amazon, Events, Polls and more.

Communication Strategies on LinkedIn

The next area I want to give attention to is the "Answers" area. This incredibly powerful component of LinkedIn gives you the ability to express your thought leadership. Part of my communications strategy is to come in at least once a month and answer a question in my areas of expertise. As you can see, you have the opportunity to ask a question that will go out to your connections or answer questions. LinkedIn generates recommended categories for you to provide answers.

You also have the option of "browsing" a list of topics and selecting the one where you'd like to review the questions to answer. Let's look at one that I recently answered in "Blogging."

Here is the question I answered: "How can you consolidate and manage all blogs, social networking (Facebook, Twitter, LinkedIn, etc.) and other online activities in one single platform?" I clicked their question and was directed to a new page.

I clicked the answer button and was able to type an answer to reply to this question. I then hit "submit." You'll see that you can also provide web addresses as resources, suggest an expert you know, and even write a direct message to this person.

After I answered the question, my name became a hyperlink that can take people back to my profile page to see my full profile. One suggestion I'd recommend, if this is a part of your communications strategy, is to set up RSS feeds for the particular categories in which you'd like to answer questions.

Search Functions within LinkedIn

LinkedIn offers an array of search functions—people, jobs, companies, and so on. You can really gather some rich data with these searches. I did one to find connections (and potential connections) in social media within fifty miles of my zip code.

My search yielded 124 results and showed how they are connected to me. Now, what if you want to connect with someone who is a 2nd or 3rd degree contact? You can look to see to whom they are linked to in your 1st degree connections. When I moved to South Carolina four years ago, I was targeting a certain company to do some contract work. I located the company on LinkedIn and was able to find out who was one of the decision-makers in the company. One of my close colleagues was her 1st degree contact.

I asked my colleague for an "Introduction" to her. Within a matter of days, she had contacted me for a networking lunch date—it was then that I really came to understand the true power of LinkedIn.

One feature I really like about LinkedIn is the "Company" search. I always encourage people to come up with a targeted list of companies for which they'd like to work when they are in a job search. You get incredible data in this area that helps you to gather the research you want to do prior to the interview. Also, you'll notice that you get information about who is in your network that currently works in the company.

Not only do you get that information, but you can also see the former employees, how they are connected to you and who their 1st degree connections are. You can see where new hires have come on board and what company they just left. Also, you can learn about who was recently promoted and from which position. Now this type of research **might** just help you to find where a potential opening has emerged.

For example, when I researched Edward Jones, I was able to find out the career paths of Edward Jones employees before and after they were employed at Edward Jones. This information might also yield data about other companies that are similar to your targeted company. Having this information might help you expand your targeted company list.

Once you've arrived on a company's page, look on the right where you find the section with **"Check Out Insightful Statistics About this Company."** Right above that hyperlink, you will see how you are connected to others at the company. However, what if you don't have any 1st degree connections (people you know personally)? You can request an introduction from a 1st degree contact and I'll show you how to do it.

First, click on the number (in my picture, it's the circled "18"):

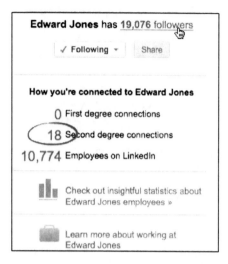

How to Request an Introduction

Once you click on the number beside the phrase, **"Second degree connections,"** you will arrive at a page that shows the pictures of those connections.

When you click on the **"8 shared connections"** (or whatever number it is for you), then you'll see the pictures and names of all the shared 1st degree connections. You can then click, **"Get Introduced"** and arrive at a screen that lists the connections with a radio button beside each name.

Select the person who knows you well and click "Continue." The next page contains the introduction. You'll type the note that you want to send to the 2nd degree connection as well as a note to your 1st degree connection. Remember to be as specific as possible as to why you are requesting the introduction and the questions you would like to ask. Close with thanking them for their time in facilitating the connection.

How to Find a Job on LinkedIn

You can also find jobs on LinkedIn. Some employers are now advertising some jobs exclusively through LinkedIn. If the job is through LinkedIn, you will only be able to apply through LinkedIn's site. On my search for "Project Manager" in South Carolina, I came up with these results:

Jobs on LinkedIn

You will be brought to a screen to show you who you know and how they are connected to you. Many times when you are reviewing the job requirements, you can look on the right-hand column and see the person who posted the position. If it is one of your connections (or a connection's connection), you can network for a warm lead. Are you starting to see the power?

You can also do more advanced job searches within the LinkedIn area for richer data.

LinkedIn Signal

LinkedIn launched "Signal" as a way to help you filter your results more quickly. This works well in filtering through status updates as well as job leads. When you run a search on a job title (i.e. project manager), notice that there is a sidebar on the left-hand side. You can refine your search results by the following:

- Radius of a ZIP code

- Relationship (1st, 2nd, and 3rd degree connections)

- Name of company—for a more targeted approach

- Date posted

- Job function

- Industry

- Experience level

For example, when I ran a search on "project manager," I returned 10,473 jobs! However, when I used the advanced search features of "Signal" and ran the search within a 100 miles of my ZIP, I got 41 results which is a much more manageable result. I then clicked "2nd degree connections" (I had no 1st degree connection results), my results dropped to 30. I then selected jobs posted in the last two to seven days and reduced the results to 14. If I had certain companies on a prospecting list where I wanted to work, such as Aflac, I would have seen that there is one position posted by that company.

LinkedIn has launched an "Apply with LinkedIn" button for company career portals that allows you as a job seeker to use your LinkedIn Profile (make sure it thoroughly completed) to apply without having to complete long application forms or try to cut and paste your resume.

Additional Communication Strategies

LinkedIn Status Update

This is a feature within LinkedIn—similar to Twitter and Face-book—that allows you to update your status. You have the ability to leave comments and "like" an update. You can also tie your Twitter account with your LinkedIn account and by checking the box beside the Twitter icon, you can ping both your LinkedIn and Twitter accounts with the update you write and share.

Recommendations on LinkedIn

Part of completing your profile is having people recommend you. You can "ask for a recommendation." Only approach people who know you very well—otherwise your request will probably be ignored. It's a good practice to write a recommendation without prompting for a person that you know well. Sometimes this will lead to them recommending you also, and at other times, you will just get a note of thanks. Interestingly, a person receiving the recommendation can choose to publish it or not. They are also able to request that you edit your recommendation to possibly include some achievement they wish to highlight. However, they CANNOT edit it themselves.

If you want to request a recommendation, then click the tab "Profile" and select "Recommendations." Here, you will choose the job or school for which you want to be recommended, choose the person (or people) to whom you want to send it, and then write your message. *Please take out the default message.* Take the time to write something personal, and tell them why you want the recommendation. If you are asking them to take this time, then you definitely want to invest the time to write something more personal than, "Can you endorse me?"

If you want to write a recommendation (and I do encourage you to make this a part of your communications plan), then click the "Sent Recommendations" tab and go to the bottom where it says, "Make a Recommendation."

Here, you will want to pick the one that is the best fit for that recommendation. Write your recommendation and submit it. The person you've vouched for will receive the recommendation and will be able to decide if they will use it on their profile or not.

For more detailed information on how to use LinkedIn to its fullest, read 'I'm on LinkedIn—Now What???' by Jason Alba (available in three editions) or check out his 'LinkedIn for Job Seekers.' The DVD (available at http://www.linkedinforjobseekers.com) is a fabulous resource because it is divided into mini-steps (approximately five minute segments) on how to leverage all the opportunities on LinkedIn.

Some additional resources include:

- **Examples of Before/After LinkedIn Profiles:**
  http://bit.ly/HcMBO3[16]

- **I'm on LinkedIn—Now What??? The Blog**
  http://imonLinkedInnowwhat.com/

Checklist for LinkedIn

1. Did you customize your LinkedIn URL? _____
2. Did you thoroughly complete all of your profile information? _____
3. Have you written a compelling summary—something that will intrigue someone to want to continue reading? _____
4. Did you complete your work history and education? _____
5. Do you have website addresses listed so that someone can click through to learn more about you? _____

---

16. imonlinkedinnowwhat.com/2012/04/03/linkedin-profile-critique-jeff-dibble/

6. Have you started inviting people to connect with you on LinkedIn by sending personalized invitations? Remember, if you use a supported platform like Gmail or Yahoo, LinkedIn can automatically pull your address book to check to see if any are on LinkedIn—if not, you can "Export" your address book to a CSV (comma separated value) and upload. _____

7. Which applications (such as blog importer for TypePad or WordPress, Slideshare, Amazon) are you going to add to your LinkedIn page?

_____

_____

_____

8. Which groups are you going to join that will help you network with people in your industry?

_____

_____

_____

9. Under the Answers section: Which topics appeal to you and will portray your expertise by answering questions? How often do you plan to answer questions (whether daily, weekly, or monthly)?

_____

_____

_____

10. What's your policy on connecting with people on LinkedIn?

_____

_____

_____

In *JibberJobber*, you can import your LinkedIn connections. Simply log in to your LinkedIn profile and export/download your LinkedIn connections into a CSV (comma separated value—MS Excel) file. Go to your JibberJobber account, mouse over the "Network" tab and select "Import/Export" to add this information into your network.

Twitter

Twitter is based in San Francisco, CA and has experienced 5000% explosive growth from 2008 to 2011.

Televised news programs and newspapers discuss the importance of Twitter in keeping people informed of up-to-date events.

To contrast, we have recently witnessed the fall of an Egyptian President and the rise to fame of a teenage singer through social media platforms. The Egyptian protest unfolded before our eyes and it was through Twitter that people were able to access real-time information as well as to keep in touch. Protests were organized via the hashtag on Twitter and the actual spark began on Facebook.

Justin Bieber was an unknown name just a few years ago. He uploaded his singing videos to YouTube and a Talent Scout, Scooter Braun in Atlanta, GA found him. Justin literally built his fan base through Twitter and within a year of producing his first single, he sold out the performance at Madison Square Garden.

Twitter is a powerful social media tool that some small to large companies use to keep on the pulse of customers' needs and wants as well as to engage in an unprecedented way with their customers. In fact, many customers expect this type of engagement. Marketers are learning how to best utilize social media to have meaningful conversations with their customers. An example of this is demonstrated in a lighthearted video, "The Break-Up" (http://www.youtube.com/watch?v=D3qltEtl7H8).

Recruiters and hiring managers are Googling potential employees prior to asking them for an interview. I have read that they will see if a candidate uses Twitter and then will review the type of information they tweet to show thought leadership and they see how they engage with others in the Twitter conversation.

Additionally, Google indexes tweets, thus making Twitter an incredibly useful online identity builder. The Library of Congress sees the information on Twitter as invaluable and are archiving tweets.

Some quick Twitter statistics provided by http://blog.kissmetrics.com/twitter-statistics/: There are 1 billion tweets per week; 572,000 accounts created on March 12, 2011 alone; the average of new accounts per day in February 2011 was 460,000!

I'm going to spend the first part of this section on how to get started on Twitter and manage your account, as it can be overwhelming for some people. I am also going to answer some of the most frequently asked questions about Twitter as someone is beginning the process. The second part of this section will discuss how you can leverage Twitter as one of the multiple strategies in your job search marketing plan.

Getting Started on Twitter

Optimizing Your Twitter Profile

After you have created an account with Twitter (http://www.twitter.com/), you will go to the top right of your home page and select "Settings." The next page will give you a menu of choices—Account, Password, Mobile, Notifications, Profile, Design, and Applications. Let's first select "Account."

Under Account, you will build information that will help people find you and find out more information about you. If you can get your own name as your user name, then this is ideal. If you own your own company and want to create a User Name for it, you can also see if that user name is available.

Try to obtain your real name as your user name as it will make it easier for people to connect with you. Capitalize the first letter of your first and last name. If you cannot get your real name, you may try a combination of ideas to get a close iteration of your name, such as Kristen_Jacoway, Kristen-Jacoway, or add something with which people attribute you, such as KristenJacowayHR.

Professional Headshot

Next, go to "Profile." You will want to upload a professional-looking headshot—people on Twitter like to see to whom they are connecting. If you do not add a picture here, Twitter will give you a default Avatar.

Website Information

You have the opportunity to include a website address in the "Web." Take advantage of this area as many will click through to your website to learn more about you prior to following you. If you don't have your own website, then you could also include your LinkedIn URL, DoYouBuzz (http://www.doyoubuzz.com) Resume link, upload your resume via a Twitter app (http://twitdom.com/twitres/), link to an article you've written, or any other link that will demonstrate your industry expertise.

One-Line Bio

Your One Line Bio is 160 characters long. Try to use keywords that people (employers, recruiters, and more) may be using to find someone like you. Research the noun and noun phrases your target companies utilize in job postings for positions in which you are interested. Those nouns and noun phrases are your clues to the keywords. Make a list and select the most commonly used keywords for people in your field and sprinkle them into your one line bio. Another resource? Go to http://www.15secondpitch.com/ to help develop your 15-second elevator pitch and then use your pitch for your Twitter Bio.

Location, Location, Location

Also, remember to add your location—you can add the city and state or just leave it as a state. Why is this important? Sometimes, employers and recruiters do what is known as a geo-targeted search to find industry professionals in a certain geographic region. If you are willing to relocate, add that information to your bio.

ACTION TIP: Make sure your bio includes the following:

1. What you do. Remember to use keywords that recruiters and employers use to find someone in your field—include the abbreviation, if applicable.

2. What are you currently working on or doing? If you are in a job search, let people know!

How to Customize Your Twitter Background

You have now registered and gone through the steps setting up some of the settings for your Twitter account. Now, you will want a background for your Twitter page. You can select one of the 19 Twitter themes that are available. If you want to have a custom background, you can create it yourself with a program such as Adobe Photoshop or by finding someone who specializes in creating custom Twitter Backgrounds.

You can Google "Custom Twitter Backgrounds" and check out the many talented designers who specialize in doing this type of work.

You are also able to change your design colors in this area. In this area, you can change your background, text, links, sidebar, and sidebar colors. I was able to use the hexadecimal numbers (i.e. 4c859e) provided by my designer to customize my colors. However, you can also use the eyedropper tool in Photoshop or a similar program to suck up the color in your picture to give you this hexadecimal number.

Additionally, you can download **ColorZilla** (http://www.colorzilla.com/firefox/) as a plug-in for your Firefox window. I sometimes use this tool when I'm on a website that a client likes to find out the hexadecimal color number for that client's site.

To use ColorZilla, simply find a color you like on a website. Click on the eyedropper tool and then double-click on the color you like. Go to the eyedropper icon on your Firefox window and double-click. A pop-up window should appear. The last box shows you the hexadecimal color number you can use to customize your Twitter background, fonts, and hyperlinked text.

Resource List for Twitter Background Designers

TwitBacks – http://www.twitbacks.com

TwitRBackgrounds – http://www.TwitRBackgrounds.com

Twitter Gallery – http://www.twittergallery.com

My Tweet Space – http://www.MyTweetSpace.com

Tweet Style – http://www.tweetstyle.com

The BrandiD – http://www.thebrandid.com

Brian Hanson – http://www.customtwit.com

Erin Blaskie – http://www.bsetc.com/

Tools within Twitter

The Art of Twitter—@Replies, Retweets, Lists, and More

You can "Mention" the follower in a tweet – this is commonly known as an "@" reply. The tweet will show up in the Twitterer's "@Connect." Make sure you are on your "Home" page to find your "@Connect" column.

How to Create a Twitter List

You can add followers to lists, i.e. social media experts, career experts, recruiters, and more. As you begin to follow people, look at their profile and their tweets—is it someone who could add value for you? If so, add them to a list. Lists make Twitter easy to navigate and engage in conversations.

If you don't have a list to match a person's expertise, simply create a list. Type in the name of the list, click to make it a public list (anyone could start following this list) or private list (many job seekers opt for this if they are in a confidential search and don't want others to see the companies or recruiters with whom they are following), and click 'Save list.'

How to Block a Follower

The next item on your drop-down selection box (where you have the ability to add someone to a list) gives you the ability to block a person. You will find that there are people who use Twitter for inappropriate reasons (Twitter will eventually find out and suspend their account). You can block that person from being able to follow you and your tweets.

How to Report a Twitterer for Spam

The last selection where you can add someone to a list gives you the ability to report a Twitterer for spam. I have used this selection a few times. I have had people write a tweet that looks like they are retweeting me, but in essence, they are providing a link that may in fact hack into the Twitterer's account that clicks through to the link. When I see people do this with my Twitter name, I immediately report them for spam. People know, like, and trust the links that I provide, so I do not tolerate someone using my Twitter username in this way.

Twitter Account Hacking and Privacy Controls

How would you know if your Twitter account has been hacked? Generally, once it's been hacked, the hacker will start tweeting out mass messages or sending out mass Direct Messages to all of your followers. Most people generally understand when they see this type of activity that your account has been hacked and you will start getting @replies telling you this information. You will need to go to your "Home" page, click "Settings," and then click the tab for Password. You will be required to type in your old password and then the new password two times. Click 'Save' to change the password.

Etiquette Tip: When someone mentions you in an @reply, make sure you do respond. For example, someone mentioned me and said "@KristenJacoway is really helpful with all things social media. Thanks so much KJ." I sent a thank you to her out in my Twitter stream and that let all of the people who follow me see her Twitter name. Some people will click through on her name to see who she is and may follow her.

One tip I will share is that **most** of the time, if you send me an @reply where you've mentioned my name (maybe a question, or a #FollowFriday recommendation), that gets my attention. I will go look at your page and visit the link you've listed for your website. Why did I say **most** of the time? The reason is that sometimes people will group lots of people together (@username, @username, @username, @username,...) and provide no explanation as to why they mentioned me with all the other people they have listed. If I'm mentioned in this type of a tweet, I don't click through to learn more. Therefore, personalize a tweet where you mention someone else.

Direct Messages are a way for people to email you on Twitter. From time to time, I will get a personal message in this area, but for the most part, they are automated messages that are sent after I follow a person (i.e., "Thanks for the follow! Interested in growing your follower following, on auto pilot? Click here: http://www.____"). I scan this area to see if there are any personal messages and delete the automated messages. Some people do not check this area at all, but I've had people DM a question to me and I do want to be open and accessible to answer their question.

TIP: Use Direct Messages or @username replies to ask someone in your Twitter network who has great reach (or what is termed sometimes as a "firestarter") to re-tweet some of your posts—especially if it is a blog post or an article you've written. Of course, choose carefully and don't bombard these people with requests. I have had many of my followers use this approach and make this request of me. This type of strategy is an excellent way to "viral market" your blog posts and article links.

I Need Followers, Now What?

Let me say that before you start trying to build a following, you will want to tweet out about 10–20 on-brand, relevant tweets that express your thought leadership and expertise (try to keep your tweets to 120 characters so that others can re-tweet you easily and give you credit—i.e., if someone re-tweets me it adds 18 characters to their tweet—RT @KristenJacoway). Why? Simply, so that when someone lands on your page, they will be able to learn more about you by scanning your public timeline. You can tweet using different types of tweets:

- Relevant article links, blog posts, etc.

TIP: Set up a Google Alerts (http://www.google.com/alerts) to catch the latest, breaking news about subjects that are going to appeal to your target audience.

People follow me for job search, entrepreneur, social media, and personal branding topics. Try to mix up your tweets, though, so that your followers don't get "click-through burnout."

- Re-tweet—a re-tweet is when you find something that another person on Twitter says and you want to repeat it. You would copy their message and then give them credit. For example, "Space Shuttle Crew fields questions via Twitter: http://www.___RT @Twittername."

- Saying or a quote—remember to always give credit to the author!

- What you are doing—you can use this opportunity to say, in a warm way, that you are looking for a job in _____ industry.

- Answer other people's questions. This is a great strategy and you can easily find people's questions through the search function. I will often use the search term "how do I" and the subject that I want to answer, for example, "how do I" and WordPress. You will get a wealth of questions that you can answer on your public timeline.

- Promotional—You see that I saved this until the last. Why? People easily get turned off if you self-promote all the time. You want to make sure that the majority of what you tweet is *not* self-promotional.

Most articles and blog posts give you the ability to share on Twitter or other social networks. Just click the icon of the social network on which you want to share the information and voila—it's sent.

Social Networking Share Buttons

Who Sees My Tweets?

A common misconception is that only your followers see your tweets. Your tweets are on a public timeline, meaning that they are searchable and anyone can see them. Additionally, many companies, hiring managers, and recruiters use "listening" tools like Google Alerts, Radian6, TweetBeep, Company Buzz (LinkedIn application), etc. to be alerted when their name or their company name has been used in social media platforms. A well-known story unfolded before the public's eyes and was recently discussed in an article, 'How Social Media Can Hurt Your Career' by Rachel Zupek (careerbuilder.com writer).[17] Here's the story:

A recent Tweet by a potential Cisco employee, for example, turned ugly when he decided to tout a recent job offer: "Cisco just offered me a job! Now I have to weigh the utility of a fatty paycheck against the daily commute to San Jose and hating the work." Unfortunately for "th-econnor" (the handle for the would-be employee), Tim Levad, a "channel partner advocate" for Cisco, saw the tweet and responded with this: "Who is the hiring manger, I'm sure they would love to know that you will hate the work. We here at Cisco are versed in the Web."

Once you post your tweet, it is much like an email. Once you hit submit, people have seen it. You may be able to delete your tweet, but the damage has already been done. Be very careful with what you post!

---

17. Rachel Zupek, "How social media can hurt your career," International CNN.com/living, August 24, 2009, http://tinyurl.com/yfjpuh9 (accessed April 29, 2012).
   edition.cnn.com/2009/LIVING/worklife/08/24/cb.job.social.medial. pitfalls

Twitter Directories

Finding people to follow is really simple and is one of the easiest ways to start getting followers for you. You can google the term, "Twitter Directories" and you'll come up with several options. Who do you want to follow? Ideally, you want to follow companies, people you've found through your research who are connected to your target companies, recruiters, job boards, and the like. I'll introduce you to a few directories:

Twellow (http://www.twellow.com) is a great place for you to list yourself in the Twitter Yellow Pages. I list myself under the following three attributes: personal branding, social media, and career consultant. Try to think of attributes to describe what you do to match what people will use in their own search to find people in those professions. What I love about Twellow is that once you've created your account and signed in, you can search and follow people all within the Twellow website.

I searched for "recruiters and healthcare" and came up with a list of people on Twitter who are recruiters in the healthcare industry. Additionally, you can search on a company's name and not only see if the company is on Twitter, but also if any employees of that company are. Again, networking is key to career transition success!

WeFollow (http://www.wefollow.com) is much like Twellow. You have to pick three tags (or attributes) that best describe you.

Twitter Grader (http://twitter.grader.com) is a fun tool. You can enter your Twitter username and come up with a Twitter grade. It measures your "power, reach, and authority" on Twitter. They have their own algorithm (or secret sauce), like Google, so they don't delve into the complete details on how they arrive at your score.

I like the "Twitter Elite" feature; this is located on the navigation bar on the right upper side of the website. Here, you can search for the "Twitter Elite" by Top Users, Top in Location, Top Cities, Top U.S. States, and Top Countries. I go here from time to time to follow people in my local area and the top users in my industry of interest. Twitter Grader makes it easy for you to find some of the leading experts in your industry.

Just Tweet It (http://justtweetit.com) is another directory where you can find people to follow and add yourself to their directory. I copied my bio from my Twitter site and inserted it here. The neat feature is you can subscribe to different directories via an RSS feed to alert you when someone new has added a profile in a directory of your interest. Then, you can check out their profile and decide if you want to follow them or not.

TweetBeep (http://tweetbeep.com/) lets you keep track of who's tweeting your website, your name, or blog. It also has the ability to know if someone has used a shortened URL (i.e., bit.ly) to talk about your website. It is truly a unique tool for online reputation management, and I've heard of people who set up these alerts on their competitors.

HootSuite 101 for Twitter Management

HootSuite is an online Twitter Management Service located at http://www.hootsuite.com. You have the option of having a free account or a paid account. I have personally been able to accomplish what I need to do with a free account; however, you may find that for your needs, the paid account would be more helpful.

Updating Multiple Social Networking Accounts

Once you have signed up for your account, you will need to link the social media accounts you want for your dashboard. You can add multiple Twitter accounts, but you can also add social media accounts from across the web. Therefore, you can update multiple social media sites from HootSuite.

To start, go to the sidebar and select "Settings" and then click "Social Networks."

A pop-up window will appear and you will have the ability to add your social networks by clicking "Add Social Network."

At this writing, you can add Twitter, Facebook, your Facebook Business Page, LinkedIn, Ping.fm, WordPress, MySpace, Foursquare, and mixi.

Once you've added the social media accounts that you want to update from HootSuite, pinging these accounts becomes a breeze (you can only have five social media accounts with the free version of Hoot-suite—if you need to update more than five accounts, you will need to upgrade to the Pro account). If I found a tweet that I think would be great for my Twitter followers, my LinkedIn Connections, my Facebook friends, and my Facebook Fan Page, then I can select these four accounts by my status update.

When I selected these four accounts, it placed a green checkmark and highlighted the picture with a blue frame. I can click **"Send Now"** to send the update out immediately or I can click the button that looks like a calendar (next to the paperclip) to **schedule the update** for a future date and time. Additionally, I can insert a URL in the box next to the button "Shrink" and use HootSuite's **URL shortner service**. HootSuite takes their URL shortner service a step further—by using this service, you can view analytics in the section of the sidebar called **"Analytics."** You can see how many people click on your URL in the tweet you sent, clicks by region, and the top referrers to your link. If you want deeper analytics, you will have to upgrade to a Pro account.

Using Twitter Lists on HootSuite

Engaging with your Twitter followers becomes a cinch with HootSuite because you can divide your page with columns that show the Twitter lists you follow. In the left-hand side under the place where you compose a status update, click "Add Stream." You will see a pop-up box appear.

When you click the tab "Lists," you will see the lists you have already created on Twitter. You can also create new lists on HootSuite.

Once you've created or chosen the existing lists you want to follow on HootSuite, your HootSuite page will be divided into columns that contain your Twitter lists. You can engage with individual Twitterers easily from these lists. Simply mouse over the right-hand area above their tweet and you can (in this order of icons) send an @reply/mention, retweet, or direct message. The arrow pointing down opens up a drop-down menu that would allow you to reply to all the people mentioned in the tweet, send the tweet as an email, or tag the tweet as a favorite.

Should I Unfollow People on Twitter?

Twitter has a rule that applies to everyone: you can follow up to 2,000 people, but until your follower ratio is at 10% less than your following, then Twitter will not allow you to follow any additional people on Twitter. Simply put, if you have followed 2,000 people, you will have to have 1,800 people follow you before you can continue to follow additional people.

I personally use a tool called Just Unfollow (http://www.justunfollow.com). You sign-in with your Twitter account and it will look at all of the people you've followed who are not following you in return. I periodically use this tool because there are people who only follow others in order to get the follow back to increase their own number of followers. They almost immediately unfollow your account. Just Unfollow makes it incredibly easy to unfollow people on their website. You can pay a very small fee per year to unfollow large numbers. For me, paying the fee was worth it because at this writing, I could only unfollow 10 people a day at the free level.

Just Unfollow has added a new feature called "Show Inactive Following." Many people start on Twitter, only to abandon their accounts, so this service is invaluable for you to identify those inactive Twitter users.

You simply click the "Unfollow" word and voila! You have just unfollowed the Twitter user who is not following you back. I will say, though, that I have about 25 people who I follow on Twitter for their expertise on different subject areas who do not follow me. I will continue to follow them because of their invaluable tweets that contain resources and tweets about trends within the industry. Simply click "Whitelist" to protect the people you want to continue to follow.

Friend or Follow (http://friendorfollow.com/) is an application where you can check to see who you are following who are not following you back.

SocialOomph (http://www.SocialOomph.com), formerly known as TweetLater, is a neat service in that you can schedule tweets into the future. When I first started with Twitter, I'd schedule old blog posts in TweetLater. I'd write "Need to Spring Clean Your Job Search Strategy?," read my blog post at _____ and it would send out the tweet on the scheduled date and time. You can also set up automated direct messages that will be sent when someone starts following you. Doing this is a matter of personal choice, but I do not recommend it. Why? Most people consider it almost spammy in nature. Let them learn about you by the way you engage with them.

Shorten URLs to Keep Your 140

Let's move on to shortening URL addresses. I am listing below a few of my favorite sites to shorten URLs. For example, my web page of http://www.kristenjacoway.com/resume-menu-and-pricing/ has 54 characters, thus eating most of my allotted Twitter characters. If I use biy.ly to shorten it, my new URL for this blog post is http://bit.ly/Jq1XiT and is only 20 characters. It's especially important to shorten URLs in Twitter given that you only get 140 characters to type your message. Cli.gs and bit.ly both have analytic tracking ability to see your click-through rate. What's a click-through rate? If you register for an account, you can look at how many people clicked the link that you tweeted.

If you are linking people to your blog, profile, DoYouBuzz, etc. in an update, this might help you to see whether or not your tweet was effective. I often tell people to journal their tweets to see how the wording affected their click-through rate. You should start to see a trend emerge on how phrasing will generate better results.

Here are the website addresses for these URL shorteners:

- http://bit.ly/ (also gives you analytics on how many people clicked through on your link)

- http://is.gd/

- http://cli.gs/ (also gives you analytics on how many people clicked through on your link)

- http://www.tinyurl.com

Recruiters and Hiring Managers on Twitter

Recruiters and hiring managers do use Twitter to look at candidates for a position. They are looking to see how you express your thought leadership and how you are engaging with others in the Twitter community. Remember, that a tweet is much like an email—you cannot undo a tweet. You can delete a tweet, but within a couple of minutes, Google has indexed the tweet. People have made many mistakes on Twitter that have cost them jobs and job opportunities. Always keep in mind that your tweets are on a public timeline. ANYONE can read your tweets, not just your followers.

Jeff Lipschultz, whom I interviewed for the "How to Work with Recruiters" section of the book, says that he uses keywords in his search to source candidates who are tweeting about the types of jobs he is trying to fill.[18] I ran a keyword search on "SAP Programming" and came up with this tweet:

Officially doing 3 programming subjects I love: Java Enterprise, .Net, and ABAP (SAP Programming).

Needless to say, this person might peak my interest to learn more about him/her.

Resources for Finding a Job on Twitter

Determine your targeted search and see if the company lists jobs via Twitter. Also, you can locate job openings by field, job type, and other criteria. Again, your search function within Twitter will be an invaluable resource to you. I could do a search on LinkedIn on retail companies in South Carolina and target a list of companies in my search. Next, I could make notes of the names of the people that are in my LinkedIn network with that company. On Twitter, I could run searches to find out if the company and/or the people working there have an account on Twitter. If they do, I could start following their tweets. I might re-tweet resources, articles, or press releases that they tweet. Maybe I'll even

---

18. Jeff Lipschultz, Principal at A-List Solutions, interviewed by Kristen Jacoway (July 28, 2009).

see them announce a job opening. By following them, though, you will have gathered (hopefully) some relevant information to discuss in an interview.

You can also search by industry or job type. When I ran a search on "pharmaceutical sales jobs," I found several listings and also potential recruiters, companies, and people to follow. At this writing, if you will scroll down on your page, you will see an RSS feed to which you can subscribe for each type of query.

Some other resources to follow (P.S. this is a "just to get you started list"—you will find many more listings on Twitter. Just didn't have space to list them all in the book):

http://twitter.com/indeed is a vertical job board.

http://twitter.com/SimplyHired is a job search agency.

http://twitter.com/microjobs connects people with new job opportunities in Twitter time and encourages employers to add a hashtag at the end of the tweet (for example, #sales, #pr) to help the job seeker find the right opportunity.

http://twitter.com/jobangels is a grassroots movement to help people find a job. It is unique because it asks you to help one person in their job search efforts by searching #jobangels. If you need help, you follow them, Direct Message @jobangels, or tweet a message with the hashtag #jobangels, so they can let others know.

http://twitter.com/SocialMediaJob is another platform to help people in their job search efforts. Employers (or anyone who has knowledge of a job opening) are encouraged to Direct Message or re-tweet job opportunities.

http://twitter.com/jobshouts is yet another job search engine.

http://twitter.com/linkup is a search engine that lists only jobs found on company websites.

Tweet My Jobs

TweetMyJobs.com (http://www.tweetmyjobs.com/) is a job board for Twitter. Go to the site and complete the free registration. You will be able to "subscribe" to job channels. Job channels are nothing more than your industry (i.e. marketing) and the geographic location.

You can follow these "channels" on Twitter and you will receive messages when a job matches your channel subscription.

TweetMyJobs gives you the ability to integrate your social media onto your profile and to link these accounts so that you can view your Facebook or Twitter connections who are connected to the company where you might want to apply. Employers and recruiters are 20 times more likely to review the resume of a referral rather than a cold lead.

You can create a searchable resume on TweetMyJobs that includes not only the typical resume components, but other areas as well. You can include this link when you tweet to answer a job posting or to give that information to employer or recruiter.

Hashtags

Probably the question I see most often among people new to Twitter center around the acronyms and the hashtag (# sign). Hashtags are how you can easily identify trending topics (#Iran Election, #FollowFriday) and is a way to find events, keywords, conferences, webinars, etc. Hashtags on Twitter place tweets in categories and gives one unique page for tweets using a certain hashtag. Envision a filing cabinet with files that are labeled and easy to access.

You can go to http://www.hashtags.org, type in your keyword, and find the relevant hashtags that support your keyword. Using hashtags also enables people with the same interest to search on a hashtag (i.e., #personalbranding) and find people who are tweeting about that subject. Hashtags helps you to connect with others who have similar interests as you, and facilitates finding people with whom to grow your network. You can search on hashtags within Twitter with their search function. Just type in the hashtag (i.e., #socialmedia) and voila! you'll find tweets of interest and people with whom you may want to connect!

I ran a search on #jobs and came up with several related hashtags. Below the tag results, you will see the latest tweets pertaining to those hashtags. Some examples include #jobs, #copywriting_job, #webprogramming_job, #mysql_job, and so forth.

I then ran a search using the keywords "hiring" and "manufacturing" and received results showing all the recent tweets listing the job posts for manufacturing positions posted on Twitter. You'll notice at the end of each tweet they usually have included an identifying hashtag of #jobs, #tweetmyjobs, and so on.

Many companies are beginning to use social media platforms and their own websites to post jobs. Why? Look at the article on '7-Eleven's New and Improved Sourcing Strategy: Will Social Media Replace Job Boards?' According to them, here's one way social media helped:

> **"Quality of Hire** - While many high-performing employees are now out of work, 7-Eleven is not receiving quality candidates from job boards. To prove this point, the Director of Talent Acquisition conducted an experiment. He decided to post one job on LinkedIn and the 7-Eleven career site rather than the job boards. In a short period of time, he received 86 quality résumés."[19]

Social media is changing the landscape of traditional job searching. I recently read an article titled 'Three Days, 20 Words, New Job' by Amy Farnsworth, where a man actually tweeted with an employee within a company and was asked in for an interview.[20] He was hired the following Monday.

Twesumes and Twininterviews are terms used on Twitter for this type of social media hiring. A twesumes is your personal bio/brand summed up in 140 characters (usually about twenty words). The technology,

---

19. Madeline Laurano, "7-Eleven's New and Improved Sourcing Strategy: Will Social Media Replace Job Boards?," Bersin & Associates, June 21, 2009, http://tinyurl.com/lyxc22 (accessed August 26, 2009). bersin.com/blog/post.aspx?id=78143fcf-2796-4392-ab40-931cfeadf381
20. Amy Farnsworth, "Three days, 20 words, new job," *The Christian Science Monitor*, August 7, 2009, http://bit.ly/L20lrN (accessed August 26, 2009). www.csmonitor.com/Business/2009/0807/three-days-20-words-new-job

according to Farnsworth, is helping to speed up the hiring process because job seekers are able to connect directly with hiring managers and recruiters.[21]

Commonly Used Acronyms on Twitter

Twitter users utilize acronyms much the same as people do when they are texting. Here are a few of the more common acronyms and the meanings associated with them (I use Google to find out meanings of acronyms!):

RT: Re-tweet

This means that you have seen a post that you would like to share with your followers. You place the RT in front of the @username to give the original person credit for the post. I prefer to say, "The Five Ways Social Media Has Changed Internet Marketing" http://www...RT @username. I find that people will click through this more often than when you lead the post with RT @username "The Five Ways...."

PRT: Partial Re-tweet or Please Re-tweet

Sometimes people will ask their followers to PRT their post—it could be for promotional reasons, charitable reasons, or something similar. Several people will just say Pls RT, though.

DM: Direct Message

When you see this, the person is referring to taking the conversation off Twitter and using the Direct Message function within Twitter.

IMHO: In My Honest Opinion

LMK: Let Me Know

F2F: Face to Face

An actual conversation in person.

---

21. Ibid.

TMB: Tweet Me Back

Request a reply.

YMMV: Your Mileage May Vary

Your experience may be different than mine.

Joining Chats on Twitter

Joining Chats: When you are launching a job search, many people have questions—i.e. best formats for resumes, what is personal branding, how to prepare for an interview, etc. Twitter has career professionals who have chats that occur on a scheduled basis. Some of the most common include #brandchat, #jobhuntchat, #careerchat, and #hirefriday.

Go to Twitter and enter in the hashtag, i.e. #jobhuntchat, on the scheduled time it meets. You will need to enter this hashtag at the end of your question or comment for it to appear real-time in the Twitter chat. Additionally, you can type in hashtags, such as #jobseekers, #jobsearch, #resume, #resumewriting, and more to see tweets that contain advice, links to articles, blog posts, resources, and more.

You can find a more detailed list of 608 (and counting!) Twitter Chats at http://bit.ly/kRE12Z.[22] The list includes the name of the chat, description, host/moderator, a hyperlink to lead you to more information, and the day/time for the chat.

Twitter is a fertile ground for forging networking connections through chats and identifying potential job opportunities. Learning how to utilize the tools available through Twitter will facilitate your job searching efforts and may be the door to open for new possibilities.

---

22. spreadsheets.google.com/spreadsheet/ccc?key=0AhisaMy
   5TGiwcnVhejNHWnZIT3NvWFVPT3Q4NkIzQVE&hl=en_US#gid=0

A great opportunity for people is to participate in chats on Twitter. You can find chats within your industry or you can attend chats to help you with your career marketing. I'm going to highlight several of the chats that may be of interest to you and then explain how a chat works on Twitter.

- **#JobHuntChat**—Every Monday from 10:00 p.m.–11:00 p.m. Eastern Time. #JobHuntChat promotes a community where job seekers, career coaches, recruiters, human resource professionals, and hiring managers can come together. Each week, #JobHuntChat focuses on six questions from job seekers and then lets real industry experts offer solutions.

- **#CareerChat**—Tuesdays at 1:00 p.m. Eastern Time.

- **#InternChat**—Tuesdays at 7:00 p.m. Eastern Time.

- **#GenYChat**—Wednesdays at 9:00 p.m. Eastern Time.

- **#HFChat**—Fridays at 12:00 p.m. Eastern Time. #HFChart is a part of #HireFriday—movement where job seekers are marketed instead of job openings.

- **#Linkedinchat**—Tuesdays at 7:00 p.m. CST. Linkedinchat covers topics about LinkedIn and leveraging this social media platform.

- **#Blogchat**—Sundays at 8:00 p.m. CST. Blogchat gives people an opportunity to discuss their blogs and gain unique insights from experts and amateurs in the field.

Basically, you will set up a column to follow the conversation on a Twitter Chat (see next section on "How to Use HootSuite in Twitter Chats"). Let's walk through an example:

Twiiter Chat

As you can see, this person posed this question on #jobhunt and #careerchat. If I wanted to provide an answer to him, I would add the "@" before his Twitter user name and answer the question followed by "#jobhunt #careerchat" so that it shows up during the live chat and other people can see my answer.

How to Use HootSuite in Twitter Chats

Following and engaging in chats on Twitter isn't as daunting as it may seem if you employ one of the Twitter management tools such as HootSuite. When I discovered Hootsuite (http://www.hootsuite.com), it really helped me to answer the question, "I have followers, now what?" Initially, after joining Twitter, I could not understand how I was going to "engage in the conversation" as everyone kept saying that you needed to do.

HootSuite provides a quick and easy way to follow chats on Twitter. Simply click on "Add Stream" and you will see a pop-up window. Next, click on "Keyword" and then type the name of the Twitter chat (make sure to use the hashtag {#} before the name of the chat). Click "Add" and HootSuite will create a new column so you can follow the tweets from that particular chat.

Creating a Twitter profile and then never doing anything to facilitate growing a strong network will yield no results. Become an active participant on Twitter and generate meaningful content for your followers. Through Twitter, I have had many opportunities to joint venture, speak, write, and provide quotes to the media.

For more information on using Twitter in your Job Search, please consider 'The Twitter Job Search Guide: Find a Job and Advance Your Career in Just 15 Minutes a Day' by Susan Britton Whitcomb, Chandlee Bryan, and Deb Dib.

How Are You Going to Use Twitter?

1. Have you completed your one-line bio, uploaded a picture, and put a website address to your blog, DoYouBuzz, LinkedIn profile, etc.? _____

2. How many results did you generate when you ran a search on your industry? _____ For recruiters in your industry? _____

3. Did you search for the targeted list of companies that you found during your research? How many of those companies are on Twitter that you can follow? _____

4. After you researched companies on LinkedIn and found names of people within your network who work at those companies, did you try to find them on Twitter? _____ If so, how many of them did you find and follow? _____

5. Have you started grouping your followers in a management tool such as HootSuite? _____ What are the group names you've assigned?

_____

_____

_____

JibberJobber allows an "Import" of my Twitter contacts. Go to the tab "Networking" and select "Import/Export." Select the tab that says "Import my Twitter Friends." You have to enter your Twitter username and password and check the appropriate button for you. Then, click "Import."

Facebook

Social networking online is a great way to reconnect with people from your past and present. I grew my network online from zero to 200+ people on Facebook in a just a couple of months. When the company for which my former husband worked closed, we sent out a message asking if anyone knew of job openings within his industry. People emailed us, direct messaged us, etc. asking for his résumé. Within one month, he'd already secured *four interviews* for different jobs. Some of the people that I network with on Facebook are friends from high school and college with whom I might never have reconnected had it not been for being able to find them on this platform.

The question I most often asked is how do you leverage Facebook in a job search. I've read that recruiters use all different types of so-cial/professional networking platforms to source clients. Therefore, if you choose to make your profile searchable, you want to make sure that you take full advantage of each social/professional networking platform to express your authentic brand. Be consistent with the information you are putting on the web so that your personal brand is clear.

1. **Copy/paste your résumé in your profile section**

   We'll talk about privacy settings in just a bit, but understand that anything that you post on the Internet may have the potential to be found. On your profile page, you can add elements from your résumé, including your work history, education, contact information, and other applicable details. You can also add website URL addresses for LinkedIn, DoYouBuzz, your website/blog, and Twitter. You can add several URL addresses, so take advantage of it.

2. **Include your elevator pitch**

   On your personal page, you have the opportunity to write your "elevator pitch" under your picture.

3. **Update your status and comment on other's status**

   Let people know *from time to time* that you are in a job search when you update your status. Some examples might include:

   - I'm looking for a position in the banking industry; does anyone know of any job leads or networking contacts in that industry?
   - I have applied for a job at XYZ company; does anyone know someone at that company?
   - I have an interview at ABC company; does anyone know someone at that company?

   I actually used the second statement once and received five emails from my Facebook friends. They all knew someone within the company and contacted their networking contact on my behalf.

   You can also comment on other people's status. I recently saw where a friend was job searching and gave her my email address so she could send me her résumé. Another friend was experiencing privacy issues with her Facebook account and I sent her the link to Nick O'Neill's article on privacy settings. Always look to see how you can help others on Facebook (or other online and offline networks).

I just wanted to point out a few things about your personal Facebook page. In this section, I've included information that I've found helpful for my personal area.

In your personal page, you can scroll down and see events on the right-hand sidebar. I pay particularly close attention to this area and ALWAYS make sure that I send birthday wishes through direct email or snail mail. It's truly one of the easiest things to do to remember people in your network!

The other tool I use is the "List" feature. I have grouped everyone according to how I know them. It's an incredibly useful tool as I can quickly open the groups and see their news feeds. Go to your profile page and click on your "Friends." You can hover over each friend's name and then hover over the "Friend" button. You will have a drop down list appear and you will be able to add that person to a particular list (some of my lists include "Auburn University," "High School Friends," "Reach Strategists," and more. I go through and comment on certain things that I find funny, interesting, amusing, and thought-pro-voking. Nothing maintains your network more than recognizing and commenting on what they are doing.

Finally, I want to provide you a link to show you how to set your privacy controls for your personal Facebook account. The full article is located at http://allfacebook.com/facebook-privacy-settings_b31836. Nick O'Neill has provided screenshots and step-by-step instructions on how to set up the types of privacy control with which you are comfortable.[23] Do you want your personal page to show up in search results? If so, the default is already checked for this area. If you want to be more private, you can uncheck this area. Additionally, *regularly* scroll to the

---

23. Nick O'Neill, "The 10 Facebook Privacy Settings You Need to Know" All Facebook, February 9, 2011, http://allfacebook.com/facebook-privacy-settings_b31836 (accessed 4/24/2012).

bottom of your Facebook page and click "Help Center" and then the link for "Privacy" for updated information on how to keep your privacy settings at the level that is right for you.

Facebook has added many new features as they are trying to support the tremendous growth they have achieved. Many experts stated that Facebook will hit 1 billion users by summer of 2012. When new features are added, new privacy features are also implemented.

Open Graph

Facebook launched a new feature in October 2011 called "Open Graph." With Open Graph, websites and apps no longer have to "ask" your permission to post your activity.

Go to your "Privacy Settings" and click on "Apps and Websites." You must go in and customize your settings to the level for which you are comfortable. Look at this picture below. When you click "Edit" by your "Apps and Websites," you can remove permission for certain features. You can also customize who sees your activity by selecting "Customize" and selecting "Only Me."

Not sure you want to go to all this trouble? Take a look at what happened in my news feed with one of my Facebook friends who had not edited settings. She read an article, 'Mother Raped Own Daughter for Sex Education' via the Washington Post Reader. Do I think my Facebook friend realized that this appeared in her friends' News Feed? Probably not.

Timeline

Timeline has officially rolled out to Facebook user pages. While Timeline is a great branding tool, it can also potentially cause privacy issues if you are not careful.

On your Timeline profile page, if you click on the middle line, you can add a "Life Event" such as a marriage, birth of a baby, college graduation, and more. However, when you click the "Save" button, look to the left of this button. The default setting is for this information to go out as a "Public" status, thereby becoming a Google result on your name.

Decide if you want this as a public or private update and set the privacy setting accordingly by clicking on the arrow to get a dropdown box of privacy choices.

TIP: Make sure your updates can pass the following tests:
1. Your update would not embarrass you if it ended up on the front page of a major newspaper
AND
2. You'd be fine with your grandmother reading it.

Default Privacy Settings

Have you set your default privacy on Facebook? You have three options:

a. Public
b. Friends and
c. Custom.

In the top right-hand corner, click the arrow button and select "privacy settings." Scroll to "Default Privacy Settings" and select the one appropriate for you. Notice that when you update your status, you can change this by clicking the arrow by the "Post" button. Then, you can change it to Public, Friends, or Custom or you can also just share with one of your lists.

Frictionless Sharing

Even if you log out of Facebook, the site can follow and track every web page you visit. Websites can write apps whereby your activity on their pages may be shared to your Facebook Profile. You can either delete every Facebook cookie in your browser or use a separate browser for Facebook (i.e. if you use Facebook on Internet Explorer, you can do your other website activity on another browser such as Firefox).

The reason for frictionless sharing is to allow online marketers to better advertise their products and services based on the websites you visit. Senator Jay Rockefeller introduced legislation in May 2011 called "Do Not Track." The legislation gained support from privacy groups, however, the online advertising industry prefers self-regulation.

Photo and Post Tagging

Facebook has rolled out a number of privacy controls on tagging people in posts, check-ins, and photos. Go to the top right side of your Timeline and beside the "Home" button, you will see an arrow that will give you a dropdown list. Select "Privacy Settings." Scroll down and select "Edit Settings" by Timeline and Tagging. You have the following options (at this writing):

- Profile Review (before a post that a friend tags you in goes on your profile, you can turn this feature on to be notified and choose whether or not you approve the tag post).

- Tag Review (friends may add tags to your post—again, this gives you the ability to approve).

- Profile Visibility (posts that you are tagged in once they are on your profile—do you want it to be public, friends only, or choose the "Custom" feature where you are the only person who sees it).

- Tag Suggestions (if this feature is on, then your friend will get a notification to tag you in photos that look like you—photo recognition).

- Friends Can Check You Into Places

I recommend you turn on all these features (except Tag Suggestions—turn this one off) to give you greater control of what gets posted about you.

As we've discussed, be very careful of what you post online because getting rid of the digital dirt may be harder than you think. People had deleted photos off Facebook thinking that the pictures were permanently deleted. PCMag.com broke a story on February 6, 2012, that reported the photos deleted by Facebook users months and even years ago remain accessible provided one has the original URL generated when the photo was uploaded to Facebook. Facebook has stated that they are working to correct this issue, but it is reported that they have known about this issue since 2009.

Job Search Apps in Facebook

Two apps have surfaced to help you utilize your Facebook connections in a job search in much the same fashion as you'd see on LinkedIn. The first app (you just search for this app and then allow it to work with your Facebook page) is called "BranchOut" and the second app is coined, "BeKnown."

Rick Marini founded BranchOut in July 2010 and touts that they are the largest job board on Facebook with 3 million+ job postings and 20,000 internships. As you search for jobs, you can leverage your Facebook friend network to foster professional relationships. For additional information on how BranchOut can help you, please visit http://branchout.com/about/productTour.

BeKnown is Monster.com's professional networking app for Facebook. Much like LinkedIn, you can search for positions and see your connections for that particular company. You can also follow companies on BeKnown to get the latest updates and news from a company. For more information on how it works, visit http://go.beknown.com/us-en/howitworks.

What's your communication strategy for Facebook?

1. BEFORE you open your account, decide your policy to "friend" people on Facebook. What's your "friend" policy? Are you going to accept all invitations or are you only going to accept invitations from close friends and family?

   _____

2. Have you set your privacy levels to a point with which you are comfortable?

   _____

3. Have you completed your personal page with the profile information and elevator pitch?

Tip: You can add your birthday, if you wish, but I would NOT include the year you were born.

Can You Pin Your Way to a Job?

What is Pinterest?

Pinterest is unlike most social media sites in that it is an interest graph versus a social graph.

Pinterest is a pinboard-style social photo-sharing website that allows users to collect images and categorize them into interest areas, such as Career Tips, Social Media, Favorite Recipes, Home Décor, and more.

Pinterest launched in closed beta in 2010 and as of April 2012, Pinterest is now the #3 most popular network behind Facebook and Twitter, according to Experian Hitwise. It gained 11.7 million unique U.S. visitors in January 2012 according to comScore, making it the fastest site ever to break through the 10 million unique visitor mark—Facebook included.

In August 2011, *Time* magazine listed Pinterest in its "50 Best Websites of 2011" article.

Have you started using Pinterest yet? If not, Pinterest might be a social media platform to check out! Pinterest is driving more traffic than Google and for someone in a job search, it may prove to give your resume a more three-dimensional view of proof of performance.

You want to make sure you can include eye-catching photographs (be careful about copyrights) that will entice someone to follow your board. I've seen people who have a board named, "Hire Me—Graphic Designer" with not only an infographic resume, but also pictures from websites that showcase their work.

Here are 7 tips for using Pinterest in a job search:

1. Fill out your Profile—click the arrow beside your name and select "Settings" to write a keyword-rich profile in the "About" section.

2. On your Settings page, give a website where a person can learn more about you. Don't have a website? Put your LinkedIn URL, Twitter URL, DoYouBuzz online resume URL, or a link to an article you've published through Ezine Articles.

3. Use keyword-rich titles and words in the Board Titles and in your descriptions. Look at Google Keyword Tool and in several job announcements that interest you and if they apply to your background and experience, sprinkle those keywords in the title and description of your pins to help people find you.

4. Tie your Pinterest account to Twitter. At this time, Pinterest only ties to your personal Facebook page, so if you have Facebook set to private, you won't be capturing outside attention to your boards.

5. Try to get your real name as your user name (under "Settings"). My vanity URL for Pinterest is http://www.pinterest.com/KristenJacoway. If you can't get your real name, try a variation such as Kristen_Jacoway or include something for which you are known after your name, such as KristenJacowayHR.

6. Find companies where you want to work to help you get a feel for the company's culture, passions, and more. This type of information can be very useful in setting you apart from other candidates in an interview. Additionally, you can use what you've learned to fine-tune and craft your cover letter that shows you've done your research about their company.

7. If you have a LinkedIn account (http://www.linkedin.com), then you can pull over your completed profile to http://www.vizualize.me into a beautiful, free infographic-type resume that you can pin to your "Hire Me" board.

Many career coaches, resume writers, personal brand strategists, social media experts, and more are using Pinterest to give advice to job seekers (myself included). A few examples include:

- http://www.pinterest.com/KristenJacoway,

- http://pinterest.com/brandspiration/,

- http://pinterest.com/marismith/

- http://pinterest.com/rwdigest/,

- http://pinterest.com/careersherpa/,

- http://pinterest.com/paulcopcutt/.

Additionally, some college career offices are also using Pinterest to give good advice, including http://pinterest.com/penncareerserv/ and http://pinterest.com/uncucs/.

Pinterest is a great place to build your personal brand online and show your thought leadership. Many blog sites now have a Pinterest social sharing icon that will allow you to share articles and blog posts in your industry of expertise. In your description, you can add relevant commentary to further demonstrate your expertise.

You can set up a "Pin It" button or "Follow Me on Pinterest" button by going to your home page on Pinterest. Select "About" and choose "Pin It Button" to get the HTML code to embed on your blog site.

Be warned: Pinterest can be addictive. It is easy to get lost in the pictorial elements of the site and realize that hours have past instead of minutes. Pinterest is one career marketing tool for your job search, but certainly there are many more tools you will use both online and offline.

Social Network Aggregator Tools

Okay, you are now on two or three social media platforms. How do you update your status quickly and easily without having to log in to each account separately? Let me introduce you to two social networking aggregating sites (you can run a Google search to find others). I'll also show you an application within Facebook that allows your post to Twitter to update your Facebook status.

HelloTxt (http://hellotxt.com/) is what I term as a social networking aggregator. It posts your status updates from their website or by using email from your mobile phone to multiple social networks. So, when I feel there is something I'd like to post to my Facebook, LinkedIn, and Twitter accounts, I update my status at this one website. It only takes me a few seconds to do and I've pinged all three of my networking websites.

Ping.fm (http://ping.fm) works much the same way as HelloTxt, posting your messages wherever you want, to more than 32+ social networking sites.

You can also add this application (http://www.facebook.com/apps/application.php?id=2231777543) to your **Facebook** page so when you update your Twitter status, you'll update your Facebook status. You will want to decide, though, if the people who are on Facebook will want to read your tweets—especially if you tweet several times per day. I personally do not use this application anymore because my Facebook personal page is for friends, family, and close colleagues. My Twitter account is more for expressing my personal brand for my business. To install it, click the "Go to Application" button and follow the instructions.

7 Resources and Tips to Use During a Job Search

Face-to-Face Networking

We've discussed many Internet strategies that you can use in your job search. However, one of the *most* important strategies that you utilize is face-to-face networking. Networking in person is probably the single most important factor in the know, like, and trust factor. You can take an online quiz at http://reachcc.com/networkquiz to find out how well you network. The reason I like this quiz so much is because all of the questions actually give you the roadmap for effective networking. For example, one question asks if you are stressed before going to a networking event or if you have taken the time to outline your objectives for the event. Preparation is definitely key to any successful networking opportunity.

Networking is actually not something you do during a career transition. If you want to be an effective networker, you do it on a daily basis. Networking's golden rule is to give more than you receive. Maintain your relationships with people —remember them on their birthdays, anniversaries, and other special occasions.

Don't just hand out your résumé and/or business card—get their information as well. Take a genuine interest in what they do. Immediately after the event, make notes about their interests, expertise, and requirements on their business card. Send them article links that they might find helpful in their profession. If you see a query on HARO (Help a Reporter Out) that they might be interested in answering, forward it to them. I've had people do this for me in the past and it really does go a long way in my wanting to reciprocate. Always be looking for ways you can help someone else.

Who comprises your network? Everyone you know from your family to your friends and colleagues. Maintain a database of everyone you know and make sure that you keep in touch with people. Facebook has been a great tool in helping me maintain relationships with people. In fact, I found out through Facebook that one of my college friends had moved within an hour's distance of me. We have now been able to see each other face to face several times.

Networking can take place at church events, Chamber of Commerce events, Business After Hours, etc. You can look in your local paper to find a detailed listing of places that are hosting networking events.

The most important tip I can give you in networking is to make sure your relationships are more give than take. Again, take a genuine interest in people—what they do, what they like, their hobbies. Doing so may open up an opportunity to show how your unique skillset may help them. One of my favorite quotes is by Epictetus: "We have two ears and one mouth so that we can listen twice as much as we speak." During my former husband's job search (both times), I've helped people in his network who were also experiencing job loss. We've given job leads to people. When you need help, helping others is a great way to network.

Some excellent books on networking include: 'Some Assembly Required' (by Thom Singer), 'Smart Networking: Attract a Following In Person and Online' (by Liz Lynch—Twitter name @liz_lynch), and 'Never Eat Alone' (by Keith Ferrazzi—Twitter name @keithferrazzi). Liz Lynch offers teleseminars and resources on her website, http://www.networkingexcellence.com/. Keith Ferrazzi's website is http://www.keithferrazzi.com.

How to Work with Recruiters

I interviewed Jeff Lipschultz from A-List Solutions (http://www.alistsolutions.com) for this section of the book.[24] Jeff is one of the principals at A-List Solutions. A-List Solutions provides management and technology recruiting along with coaching on personal branding and social media practices for proactive career branding. In the interview, we discussed tips on working with a recruiter, myths people have about recruiting, what elements of a résumé get it to the top of the pile, and how recruiters leverage social media platforms to find candidates.

I asked Jeff for his top tips for working with recruiters:

- Build a strong bond of trust with the recruiter. Find a recruiter who will take time to work with you. Be completely open and honest with them. Remember, the recruiter is placing his/her reputation on the line when they refer a candidate for a position. For example, if a person tells a recruiter that they are willing to take a certain salary, but then goes in to the interview and says otherwise, it will impact the relationship with the recruiter.

- Listen to the recruiter's advice/input. The recruiter has an established relationship with the company and understands their expectations and the personalities involved in the process. This knowledge can prepare you for applying, interviewing, negotiating salary, and other situations that may arise. A good recruiter will work with you throughout the process, right to the end. Even if you've been told by someone else to do X with your résumé, listen to the recruiter representing the company. The recruiter knows what the company wants to see. (Again, this goes back to customizing your résumé for each position for which you are applying to demonstrate how your skills and abilities are a good fit for the company).

- Continually share your thoughts throughout the process. Communicate your level of interest about the position as it might prompt a discussion to mitigate any concerns you might have about the company or the position.

---

24. Jeff Lipschultz, Principal at A-List Solutions, interviewed by Kristen Jacoway (July 28, 2009).

- Build a lifetime relationship with two good recruiters in your industry. Remember networking's golden rule: GIVE. How? You can help a recruiter by recommending them to fill positions within a company and you can also give recommendations of strong candidates you know that might be interested in the job openings that the recruiter is trying to fill. Stay in touch and keep them updated from time to time about you—have you been promoted, laid off, learned new tools. Also, ask how the recruiter is doing, invite him/her out for coffee once in a while—maintain the relationship as you would with anyone in your network.

I asked Jeff to explain how recruiters work with people in a job search. The biggest myth I hear from people with whom I work is that if they can just get their résumé in the "golden" hands of a recruiter, they can let the recruiter find them a job. Jeff explained that getting placed depends on the job openings that the recruiter is trying to fill. Recruiters do want good candidates and their résumés because sometimes they will see a match (with their current or future projects) and can eventually place you. However, a recruiter is not looking for a job for you, but rather filling the needs for the company.

Jeff also shared the top three secrets that will get your résumé to the top of their pile:

- Recruiters are looking for career progression—an increase in responsibility and/or complexity of assignments over a period of time. As a career progresses, successful people take on new roles or harder projects.

- Recruiters also appreciate seeing that you have demonstrated a willingness to learn new things. This can include new industries, tools/skillsets, processes, or roles. Companies like hiring candidates who understand the challenges associated with that job, whether it is working with their type of clients/vendors or industry-related. They like having a candidate who is ahead on the learning curve because that quality saves everyone time.

- Recruiters want a well-written and formatted résumé. Your résumé is the first impression (the majority of the time) that recruiters and employers have of you. The quality of the résumé is part of the image that you are projecting about your work. Poor quality equals a poor impression.

- **Bonus:** You should be passionate about your role. People who are passionate can tell you what's happening in their field—the latest news, books, articles, and other related information. Having enthusiasm and zeal for what you do and showing it helps to tip the scales in your favor or differentiate you.

Lastly, Jeff and I also discussed how recruiters use Twitter, LinkedIn, and blog platforms to find qualified candidates for positions. Recruiters can search within Twitter using industry keywords to find people who are tweeting about topics related to the industry for which they recruit. Recruiters also engage their followers in tweets by asking, "Do you know someone that meets the job requirements of XYZ?"

Jeff recommends that you let Twitter be the billboard to your blog. He shared a story about one of his candidates who he advised to start a blog. Jeff asked the candidate to Direct Message him on Twitter when he launched a blog post and he would re-tweet the link to the blog post (this is a great strategy). The candidate used this strategy and Jeff re-tweeted the link. 'The Wall Street Journal' actually picked up one of his blog posts, liked it, and contacted the candidate for permission to use it in their online newspaper. A few weeks later, the candidate had secured a new position because of the exposure he'd received.

Jeff is very interested in candidates with a blog as it gives a dimension to the person that a résumé cannot. A well-written blog about a person's field of expertise shows the passion and the knowledge one has about his/her industry. Jeff also added that many recruiters use LinkedIn profiles as a searchable online résumé. In this profile, one can also highlight their blog posts.

In closing, developing a lifelong relationship with your recruiter(s) is very important. You want your recruiter to know, like, and trust you. As with anyone in your network, you want to GIVE to your recruiter to solidify the relationship.

*You can maintain a database of the recruiters with whom you are working on **JibberJobber**. Go to "Companies" and select "Recruiters" to add in the details.*

Thousands of Job Boards—How Do I Choose?

Finding a one-size, fits all job board is almost impossible. Thousands of job boards exist these days, so how does one choose? Vertical job boards aggregate job postings from other job boards and can provide you with job postings from multiple job boards, including CareerBuilder, Monster, TheLadders, and Execunet.

I recently read an article by Eric Shannon where he lists the top vertical job boards for 2009.[25] (P.S. I researched to see which of these are active on Twitter and listed them in the Twitter section):

- http://www.indeed.com

- http://www.simplyhired.com

- http://www.topusajobs.com

- http://www.juju.com

- http://www.job-search-engine.com

- http://www.careerjet.com

- http://www.gojobs.com

- http://www.jobalot.com

- http://www.getthejob.com

- http://www.linkup.com

---

25. Eric Shannon, "Top job search engines - the list," InternetInc.com, August 15, 2009, http://www.internetinc.com/?s=top+job+search (accessed August 26, 2009).

You might want to try researching niche job boards in your industry. I ran a Google search on "Manufacturing Job Boards" and returned several results. I even found a niche job board for "Manufacturing Jobs for Women."

My best suggestion with job boards is not to spend all your time with your job marketing here. Set up RSS feeds and email alerts to let you know when a position posts in that meets your search criteria. I know many people who spend their entire day applying to jobs online while neglecting to use other strategies in their job search. Job boards are an important piece. However, I hope the point you remember from this book is it takes **multiple** strategies to be effective in your job search.

Company Websites

Once you have a targeted list of companies where you want to work, visit their website. Do they have a place where you can apply for a position directly on their website? If so, I'd encourage you to apply for the positions for which you are qualified here on their website. When you apply on their website, it demonstrates that you at least have some knowledge of what their company does. When you apply on a job board, then you are staying within that job board's website.

Many companies offer the ability for you to set up email alerts on the type of position for which you are seeking, which office location, etc. When you have this ability, definitely subscribe to it, as it will automate the process for you by only feeding you the jobs in which you are interested via your email.

Professional Trade Journals

Subscribe to Professional Trade Journals within your industry. Many list job opportunities that are not found in other places. I have actually secured two full-time contract positions by using this strategy. Find out if you can submit articles to these trade journals in your industry. Doing this may not increase your visibility online (as many of these journals are for subscribers only), but will increase your visibility and thought leadership to people who are in your target audience.

Interviews

Of course, you want to prepare for your interviews by doing your due diligence on the company. However, what is good research? Is it enough to know what a company does, their philosophy, and company culture? Or, do you need to dig deeper to really help position yourself as a memorable candidate?

Naturally, you have read enough to know what the company does, but I contend that companies really want to see how you are going to facilitate solutions to the challenges that they are facing. I suggest you conduct a SWOT analysis on the company prior to your interview. SWOT analysis is a method to evaluate Strengths, Weaknesses, Opportunities, and Threats and the technique is credited to Albert Humphrey. Let's look at some questions you might use in this type of research on a company:

Strengths

1. After reviewing articles in the industry, looking at your own first-hand knowledge of the company, and reviewing their last three years of revenue (if they are a public company, you'll be able to find this type of information easily—if they are private, it may be more difficult to obtain), what do you see as the company's strengths?

_____

_____

_____

_____

2. Is the company in growth mode or are they experiencing a decline in revenues?

_____

_____

_____

_____

3. What are the attributes that set the company apart from their competition? Do they excel in customer service, lead sales with a particular product, etc.?

_____

_____

_____

_____

4. How does the company position itself? What is their reputation in the marketplace? Does it align with their core message?

_____

_____

_____

_____

5. How is their online visibility? Where do you find the company? Are they on Twitter, LinkedIn, have a blog, website, or any other platform? If so, are they actively using their online tools to market their presence? Did you find any reviews from customers about them? If so, were they positive or negative?

_____

_____

_____

_____

6. Is/Are there any achievement(s) which the company is proud of? For example, have they achieved 1 million man hours without a lost time accident, breaking a sales record, first to develop a type of product, leader in their industry, etc.

_____

_____

_____

_____

Weaknesses

1. Based on your research, are they missing any opportunities to position themselves with online platforms? If so, which ones do you think would best support the company's objective?

_____

_____

_____

2. Are they in a period of decline in revenues? If so, why?

_____

_____

_____

_____

3. What attributes of the company or people working for the company may be leading to any of the weaknesses that you have uncovered?

_____

_____

_____

4. What do you perceive to be the company's weaknesses?

_____

_____

_____

5. Is there a program, product, or service that didn't fulfill the company's objective? What was it and why does the company feel that it was not a success?

_____

_____

_____

Opportunities

1. In what areas of the company do you see growth potential? What programs, policies, services, principles, procedures, and plans might best facilitate that growth?

_____

_____

_____

_____

2. What internal/external opportunities and/or resources exist that will support growth for the company?

_____

_____

_____

3. Will the company's target market support this type of opportunity?

_____

_____

_____

Threats

1. Who are the company's top three competitors?

_____

_____

_____

2. Have any of the company's competitors captured market share away from the company? If so, how much and why?

_____

_____

_____

_____

3. What are some of the challenges the company is currently facing?

_____

_____

_____

4. What is the economic climate of the company?

_____

_____

_____

5. Is the company experiencing high turnover in different positions?

_____

With this said, tread lightly on voicing your opinion about their weaknesses and threats. Remember, you are still an outsider to this company. Focus on their strengths and opportunities. Show you can innovate the ideas to facilitate the opportunities.

Now, for the other interview questions. You can expect probably six categories that your interviewer will ask:

1. **Rapport-building questions** – redirect on any subject that might be controversial, though. Mainly, they want to see your water cooler personality.

2. **Résumé-related questions** – they may use this opportunity to gain further clarification on any part of your résumé.

3. **Qualifications for the job in question** – you can expect to be asked how your skills and abilities make you the perfect candidate for the job. Be sure to know the job posting well enough that you already can answer these questions.

4. **Behavioral questions** – my position on behavioral interviewing questions is to know your achievements like the back of your hand. Why? Because most behavioral interviewing questions are going to center around telling them about a time that you had to do xyz and what was the result. Think of different types of scenarios they could ask—maybe a time when you worked under stress, or a time when you disagreed with your boss and the outcome.

Match your achievement stories with this type of scenarios. Why do they ask these questions? To see how you might perform in future tasks based on what you did in the past.

5. **Case/Situation questions** – case questions might include giving you a current challenge the company is facing and asking you how you would solve it. If you've done the SWOT analysis, you'll be well prepared for these questions.

6. **Personality questions** – such as, if you could be a tree, what kind of a tree would you be and why? They are usually assessing how quickly you think on your feet.

Now, it's your turn. The interviewer will ask you if you have any questions and you definitely want to have formulated questions that you will ask based on your research and curiosity about the company. The one question I'd encourage you to ask at the very end is: "I'm very interested in this position (if you are)—will you be contacting me or would you prefer that I contact you?" If they ask for you to contact them, make sure you set a date of when you will follow up.

For more information and a good resource, visit http://www.interviewangel.com. You can order a padfolio or a down-loadable pdf that includes: 5 Ways to Inspire the Hiring Manager to Offer You the Job; Critical Preparation Worksheets; Essential Checklists for Phone and In-Person Interviews; and Key Interview Templates to Use During the Interview. My favorite part? For every customer purchase at the standard non-discounted price, an equal donation of Interview Angel will be made to charities providing career services to those in need.

*You can list out some possible interview questions and your answers to those questions in **JibberJobber**. Go to "Interview" and select "Add" under "Question/Answer."*

Chapter 7: Resources and Tips to Use During a Job Search

8 Conclusion

I sincerely hope that the information in this book has you well on your way to a successful career transition.

I realize that you may wonder what you might do during this time. Take time to evaluate where you want to be when you retire. What classes you might take to help you reach this goal?

One emerging field is sustainability/green jobs. Indeed.com has a chart published in August 2009 that demonstrates the incredible rise of "green"/"sustainability" jobs.[26] From 2005 to 2009, there has been a greater than 600 percent increase in these types of job. Interestingly, prior to July 2005, Indeed shows that these types of job postings were not available.

The recent economic stimulus bill included $500 million for "green jobs" training, according to an article written by Kent Hoover of the 'Dayton Business Journal.' In the article, Mr. Hoover

---

26. Indeed, "Sustainability Job Trends," Indeed, August 2009, http://indeed.com/jobtrends?q=Sustainability&l= (accessed August 26, 2009).

reports "priority will be given to training programs that target low-income workers, the unemployed, and high school dropouts in areas with high poverty rates."[27]

In the book, 'Green Jobs: A Guide to Eco-Friendly Employment,' written by A. Bronwyn Llewellyn, James P. Hendrix, and K.C. Golden, the authors discuss how this "green wave holds significant implications for the future of jobs and careers."[28]

The majority of companies are showing an interest in their "carbon footprint" and taking initiatives to change. My recent Google search found 121 million results for the term "Green Companies."

To find green jobs, you may want to visit these websites: http://www.ecojobs.com, http://www.greenenergyjobs.com, and http://www.greenjobs.com.

Whether you are following the same career direction or reinventing yourself for a new direction, the steps outlined in this book will increase your visibility and reach to the people who are integral to your success. Take the time to research, outline your goals, and the steps you need to attain those goals so you can reach new heights. Remember you are in charge of your career management, so implement these strategies on an ongoing basis so that you are always prepared for change.

---

27. Kent Hoover, "U.S. to award 'green jobs' training grants in June," *Dayton Business Journal*, May 1, 2009, http://dayton.bizjournals.com/dayton/stories/2009/05/04/story7.html (accessed August 26, 2009).
28. A. Bronwyn Llewellyn, James P. Hendrix, and K.C. Golden, *Green Jobs: A Guide to Eco-Friendly Employment* (Avon: Adamsmedia, 2008).

Complete Bibliography

Alba, Jason. *I'm on LinkedIn—Now What???* *Second Edition.* Cupertino: Happy About, 2008.

Alba, Jason. "Social Media Success Summit." May 2009.

Arruda, William, and Kirsten Dixson. *Career Distinction: Stand Out by Building Your Brand.* Hoboken: John Wiley & Sons, 2007.

Blaskie, Erin, Owner of Business Services, ETC. and The VA Coach, interviewed by Kristen Jacoway. (July 31, 2009).

Comm, Joel. *Twitter Power: How to Dominate Your Market One Tweet at a Time.* Hoboken: John Wiley and Sons, 2009.

Cross-tab Transforming Market Research, "Online Reputation in a Connected World," January 2010, http://tinyurl.com/7vfv279 (accessed April 29, 2012).

Farnsworth, Amy. "Three days, 20 words, new job." *The Christian Science Monitor*, August 7, 2009, http://bit.ly/L20lrN (accessed August 26, 2009).

Hoover, Kent. "U.S. to award 'green jobs' training grants in June." *Dayton Business Journal*, May 1, 2009, http://dayton.bizjournals.com/dayton/stories/2009/05/04/story7.html (accessed August 26, 2009).

Indeed. "Sustainability Job Trends." Indeed, August 2009, http://indeed.com/jobtrends?q=Sustainability&l= (accessed August 26, 2009).

iProspect. "iProspect Blended Search Results Study (2008)." iProspect, April 2008, http://tinyurl.com/yjc8chf (accessed August 26, 2009).

Jobvite. "2011 Social Recruitment Survey Results." Jobvite, http://recruiting.jobvite.com/resources/social-recruiting-survey.php (accessed April 24, 2012).

Laurano, Madeline. "7-Eleven's New and Improved Sourcing Strategy: Will Social Media Replace Job Boards?" Bersin & Associates, June 21, 2009, http://tinyurl.com/lyxc22 (accessed August 26, 2009).

LinkedIn Customer Service Center. "Removing a Connection." LinkedIn, http://tinyurl.com/ykl355t (accessed April 23, 2012).

LinkedIn. "About Us." LinkedIn, http://press.linkedin.com/about (accessed April 23, 2012).

—. "Management." LinkedIn. http://press.linkedin.com/management (accessed April 29, 2012).

Lipschultz, Jeff, Principal at A-List Solutions, interviewed by Kristen Jacoway (July 28, 2009).

Llewellyn, A. Bronwyn, James P. Hendrix, and K.C. Golden. *Green Jobs: A Guide to Eco-Friendly Employment*. Avon: Adamsmedia, 2008.

O'Neill, Nick. "The 10 Facebook Privacy Settings You Need to Know."
All Facebook, February 9, 2011,
http://allfacebook.com/facebook-privacy-settings_b31836 (accessed
April 25, 2012).

Shannon, Eric. "Top job search engines - the list." InternetInc.com,
August 15, 2009, http://www.internetinc.com/?s=top+job+search
(accessed August 26, 2009).

Sullivan, Jennifer. "Nearly 15 Percent of Hiring Managers Would
Dismiss a Candidate Who Doesn't Send a Thank-You Letter, Career-
Builder.com Survey Finds." PR Newswire, August 16, 2005,
http://tinyurl.com/ybgdlyh (accessed August 26, 2009).

Toynbee, Arnold. "Quotations by Author." The Quotations Page,
http://www.quotationspage.com/quotes/Arnold_Toynbee/ (accessed
August 26, 2009).

Wikipedia. "Mary McLeod Bethune." Wikipedia. August 25, 2009.
http://en.wikipedia.org/wiki/Mary_McLeod_Bethune (accessed August
26, 2009).

YouTube. "YouTube Fact Sheet." YouTube.
http://youtube.com/t/press (accessed April 20, 2012).

Zupek, Rachel. "How social media can hurt your career." International
CNN.com/living, August 24, 2009, http://tinyurl.com/yfjpuh9 (accessed
April 29, 2012).

Appendix A: Complete Bibliography

Resources

I've listed 100+ resources throughout the book and wanted to include a section with all of these resources in one, easy-to-find place. So here it is:

Books

1. 'The How of Happiness' by Sonja Lyubomirsky

2. 'The 4:8 Principle: The Secret to a Joy-Filled Life' by Tommy Newberry

3. 'Career Distinction: Stand Out by Building Your Brand' by William Arruda and Kirsten Dixson

4. 'Strengthsfinder 2.0' by Tom Rath

5. 'I'm on LinkedIn—Now What???' by Jason Alba (available in two editions)

6. '2500 Keywords to Get You Hired' by Jay Block

7. 'Best Keywords for Resumes, Cover Letters, and Interviews' by Wendy Enelow

8. 'Some Assembly Required' by Thom Singer

9. 'Smart Networking: Attract a Following In Person and Online' by Liz Lynch

10. 'Never Eat Alone' by Keith Ferrazzi

11. 'Green Jobs: A Guide to Eco-Friendly Employment' by A. Bronwyn Llewellyn, James P. Hendrix, and K.C. Golden

12. 'The Twitter Job Search Guide: Find and Advance Your Career in Just 15 Minutes a Day' by Susan Britton Whitcomb, Chandlee Bryan, and Deb Dib

Career Management Resources

* http://www.jibberjobber.com
* http://twitter.com/jasonalba

Personal Branding Resources

* http://www.reachpersonalbranding.com
* http://www.onlineidcalculator.com
* http://www.reachcc.com/360v5register
* http://www.reachbrandingclub.com
* http://www.thepersonalbrandingblog.com
* http://www.google.com/alerts
* http://twitter.com/reachbranding
* http://twitter.com/williamarruda
* http://twitter.com/kirstendixson
* http://www.reputation.com

Resources for Publishing Articles

* http://www.ezinearticles.com
* http://twitter.com/skydiver
* http://www.helpareporter.com

Popular Blogging Platforms

* http://www.wordpress.com
* http://www.wordpress.org
* http://www.typepad.com
* http://www.blogger.com

Resources for Blog/Website Hosting

* http://www.godaddy.com
* http://www.bluehost.com
* http://www.dreamhost.com
* http://www.mediatemple.com
* http://www.justhost.com
* http://laughingsquid.us/

Resources for Your Blog

* http://labs.wordtracker.com/seo-blogger/
* http://www.youtube.com/watch?v=kuVqFyEtEFM
  How to Insert Video into Your Blog
* http://www.problogger.net
* http://www.problogger.net/31dbbb-workbook/
* http://www.technorati.com
* http://twitterfeed.com
* http://www.gravatar.com
* http://www.alltop.com

Video Resources

* http://www.youtube.com
* http://www.ustream.tv
* http://www.techsmith.com

- http://www.jingproject.com
- Flip or Flip Mini HD camera
- iMovie for Mac - editing
- Windows MovieMaker - editing
- http://www.videobio.com
- http://videobio.com/page/products

Research Tools

- http://www.simplyhired.com/a/jobtrends/home
- http://www.zoominfo.com

Profiling Platforms (Examples)

- http://www.google.com/profiles
- http://www.linkedin.com
- http://www.spoke.com
- http://www.ziggs.com
- http://www.ecademy.com

LinkedIn Resources

- http://www.linkedin.com/
- http://www.LinkedInforJobSeekers.com
- http://imonLinkedInnowwhat.com/

Facebook Privacy Link

- http://allfacebook.com/facebook-privacy-fix-timeline_b75559

Résumé Resources

- http://www.hoovers.com
- http://www.wendyenelow.com/bookstore.php
- http://www.parw.com/home.html
- http://online.onetcenter.org/find
- http://www.doyoubuzz.com
- http://twitdom.com/twitres/

Vertical Job Boards

- http://www.indeed.com
- http://www.simplyhired.com
- http://www.topusajobs.com
- http://www.juju.com
- http://www.job-search-engine.com
- http://www.careerjet.com
- http://www.gojobs.com
- http://www.jobalot.com
- http://www.getthejob.com
- http://www.linkup.com

Green/Sustainability Job Boards

- http://www.ecojobs.com
- http://www.greenenergyjobs.com
- http://www.greenjobs.com

Job Boards on Twitter

- http://twitter.com/indeed
- http://twitter.com/SimplyHired

- http://twitter.com/microjobs
- http://twitter.com/jobangels
- http://twitter.com/SocialMediaJob
- http://twitter.com/jobshouts
- http://twitter.com/linkup
- http://www.TweetMyJobs.com

Networking Resources

- http://www.reachcc.com/networkquiz
- http://www.networkingexcellence.com/
- http://www.keithferrazzi.com
- http://www.15secondpitch.com/new/

Business Card Resources

- http://www.vistaprint.com
- http://us.moo.com/en/

Shortened URL Resources

- http://bit.ly/
- http://is.gd/
- http://cli.gs/
- http://www.tinyurl.com

Twitter Directories

- http://www.twellow.com
- http://www.wefollow.com
- http://twitter.grader.com
- http://justtweetit.com

Resources for Customizing Twitter Backgrounds

- TwitBacks – http://www.twitbacks.com
- TwitRBackgrounds – http://www.TwitRBackgrounds.com
- Twitter Gallery – http://www.twittergallery.com
- My Tweet Space – http://www.MyTweetSpace.com
- Tweet Style – http://www.tweetstyle.com
- The BrandiD – http://www.thebrandid.com
- Brian Hanson – http://www.customtwit.com
- Erin Blaskie – http://www.bsetc.com/
- http://tinyurl.com/m3j9ba
- http://www.colorzilla.com/firefox/
- http://addons.mozilla.org/en-US/firefox/addon/539

Miscellaneous Twitter Resources

- http://tweetbeep.com/
- http://friendorfollow.com/
- http://www.SocialOomph.com
- http://www.hashtags.org
- http://www.hootsuite.com
- http://www.justunfollow.com

Social Media Aggregator Tools

- http://hellotxt.com/
- http://ping.fm
- http://www.facebook.com/apps/application.php?id=2231777543

Erin Blaskie (Interview on Video)

* http://www.erinblaskieinc.com
* http://twitter.com/erinblaskie

Jeff Lipschultz (Interview on Recruiters)

* http://www.alistsolutions.com
* http://alistsolutions.com/wordpress/
* http://twitter.com/jlipschultz

Updated Resources and Additional Information

* http://twitter.com/KristenJacoway
* http://www.facebook.com/CareerDesignCoach
* http://www.pinterest.com/KristenJacoway
* http://pinterest.com/brandspiration/
* http://pinterest.com/marismith/
* http://pinterest.com/rwdigest/
* http://pinterest.com/careersherpa/
* http://pinterest.com/paulcopcutt/
* http://www.job-hunt.org/

About the Author

Kristen Jacoway was the Assistant Editor for 'YOUnique' (a global newsletter reaching 45,000+ subscribers), and her work as a contributing writer is featured in 'Cover Letters for Dummies,' 3rd edition, by Joyce Lain Kennedy (Wiley Publishing, January 2009), and 'Personal Branding for Dummies' by Susan Chritton (Wiley Publishing, June 2012). She has been recently quoted in Monster.com, TheLadders.com, and Aol, and is a career columnist for the Atlantic City Weekly. Career Rocketeer named her as one of the 150+ Experts on Twitter All Job Seekers Must Follow.

Kristen earned her BS and MS degrees in Vocational Counseling from Auburn University. Her professional credentials include:

- Certified Personal Brand Strategist

- Certified Career Coach

- Certified Rehabilitation Counselor

- Certified Professional Résumé Writer

- Certified Employment Interview Professional

- Certified Online Identity Specialist

Other Happy About® Books

Purchase these books at Happy About http://happyabout.com or at other online and physical bookstores.

I'm at a Networking Event—Now What???

Through this book you will learn how to make quality connections, cultivate relationships, expand your circle of influence through networking events, and create good "social capital."

Paperback: $19.95
eBook: $14.95

Storytelling about Your Brand Online & Offline

This book covers the gamut of online and offline opportunities available to tell the story about the "Brand Called You" to your target in a compelling way.

Paperback: $22.95
eBook: $16.95

I'm on LinkedIn—Now What???

This book explains the benefits of using LinkedIn and recommends best practices so that you can get the most out of it.

Paperback:$19.95
eBook:$14.95

Happy About My Resume

The book will help readers learn how to quickly create a resume that is professional, gets them noticed, minimizes the amount of time they spend in a job search, and maximizes their earning power.

Paperback: $19.95
eBook: $14.95

More Praise for I'm in a Job Search—Now What???

"As a person employed with the State of Alabama to help people find jobs, I know how frustrating it is to send résumé after résumé with no results. Job seekers today need compelling ways to set themselves apart. Kristen Jacoway delineates such concepts as personal branding and managing your digital footprint, techniques that are both powerful and timely. With her sensible strategies, Kristen has enhanced my professional and personal approach to employment seeking."
Bedarius Bell Jr., State Coordinator of Deaf and Hard of Hearing Services

"Although I'm not job searching, this book is a page-turner. Kristen breaks down the daunting job search process into something interesting, compelling and enjoyable. Her writing style makes you feel as if she is right next to you coaching you along. The 21st-century job search tips and tools in this book are priceless. A must read for ANYone searching for a new job or career!"
Rachel Gogos, President, brandiD, http://www.thebrandid.com

CPSIA information can be obtained at www.ICGtesting.com
Printed in the USA
LVOW13s1323091013

356171LV00007B/32/P

9 781600 052262